KWEER SKEETER

By:

T C LUTHER

Contents

Dedication 1

Acknowledgments 2

About the Author 3

Chapter One 5

Chapter Two 23

Chapter Three 49

Chapter Four 66

Chapter Five 69

Chapter Six 81

Chapter Seven 98

Chapter Eight 108

Chapter Nine 116

Chapter Ten 121

Chapter Eleven 153

Chapter Twelve 158

Chapter Thirteen 169

Chapter Fourteen 189

Chapter Fifteen 219

Chapter Sixteen 226

Chapter Seventeen 245

Dedication

This is the second written work created on a new journey that I recently began due to the devastating loss of my mother to a sudden illness a short while ago.

Again, I dedicate this to my loving mother, whose passing has forever reminded me that life is short and you only have yourself to blame if your life ends and you have regrets. As Mom would frequently say, "You don't get do-overs, so live your life to its fullest."

I love you, Mom, and I follow your wisdom.

Acknowledgments

A special thank you goes to all the special people in my life who make up my "family." You know who you are.

Thank you for your continued support as I navigate this exciting new literary journey.

About the Author

T.C. Luther began life in a large, bustling city on the West Coast of the United States, but at an early age, he was relocated to a small plot of land in a rural community in the Midwest. T.C.'s parents were hard workers and ran a small family farm in their free time. There was little time for socializing with other kids or relatives, and the family wasn't wealthy, so going out on the town was almost unheard of.

When not in school, T.C. spent much of his time busy performing chores around the farm that were required by his parents to help the family put food on the table. In his free time, with minimal outside interaction, T.C. spent much time alone fantasizing and creating unique worlds where his mind and spirit could soar and escape the confines of that Midwestern farm.

T.C. has a lifelong interest in learning and academics, focusing mainly on history and the fine arts. This interest led him to complete degrees in the creative arts with backgrounds in architecture and history. Over his lifetime, the desire for learning took T.C. from the Midwest to the South and even as far east as Philadelphia and New York City, where he gained worldly knowledge and experienced a much quicker pace of life, seeing how the other half lives.

Having spent time in the Big Apple and growing weary of the hustle and bustle, T.C. returned, a few years ago, to his origins on the West Coast, stating his West Coast roots have called for him to return home his entire life, and he finally decided to listen. Here, he has found contentment and strives to live a life enriched with the beauty and creativity his active mind creates for him and those around him.

Chapter One

Mosquitoes are a real nuisance, and most of us have had one or more experiences with them in our lifetime. Point out anyone who has not been the victim of a mosquito bite, and I'll be the first to tell them they should be in a museum so we can study their unique life experience.

I know mosquitoes are just as necessary to the environment as everything else, but I don't like mosquito bites. They are annoying, what with the initial numbing, stinging, and burning, and then having to deal with the bite area swelling. Then there's the intolerable, never-ending itch that can sometimes take forever to go away. The experience can take control of your life for days. A simple and standard set of symptoms, right? Most of the time, yes.

Let me tell you about when I was bitten by one or more of those damned bloodsuckers that forever changed my life.

The name is Tom, Tom Broadmore. I work for a large land survey company located in Central Florida. Because of the amount of business generated by clients who need to have their properties surveyed, our company has set up dedicated teams who generally work together from one project to the next.

After some research, our company determined it was more efficient to employ teams or survey crews who worked together on multiple projects with the hope that this would help develop that team spirit and camaraderie that promised to keep workers motivated and even excited to work together and hard as a "team." It was like creating a "family" away from their regular family.

This worked well when a project arose where the team needed to be away from their regular family and would spend working days and restful evenings with their "work family," camping out at a remote site.

Having worked in land surveying for most of my adult life, I have transitioned from the low man on the proverbial totem pole and am now the Chief Surveyor for my crew. The number of crew members on a survey team varies, depending on the scope of the project and the project deadline.

My team consists of 4 members, including me.

My assistant is Brent. He's been with our company for a few years now and has proven his ability to complete any task and do it efficiently. I have worked with him for several years as a dedicated team member. I rely upon Brent to help our team complete any projects assigned to us. He has helped relieve my stress to perform and produce the work required on time.

Brent is my right-hand man. He has learned under me, and I've helped him become a competent land surveyor; he's ready to move up to Chief Surveyor, and I'm confident he will soon be in charge of his own team. He's a great guy and always willing to please.

Rounding out our four-member team are Roger and Cliff. Roger and Cliff are considered "rod men" on our team. Roger is the official "rodman." The rodman on a survey crew is responsible for holding what surveyors call a prism, a mirrored glass object attached to the top of a telescoping poll.

The chief surveyor will input coordinates into the scope or the equipment used to "shoot" or record coordinates. Once all required coordinates have been recorded during a typical survey, these coordinates are taken back to the office. A drafting team will translate the field measurements and coordinates into highly detailed and accurate survey drawings. Those drawings can vary in detail depending on the information required by law or the client's request. For example, some surveys focus on a small parcel of land and may or may have to show buildings and any other improvements or land formations on that property. Those drawings are usually called plats. However, another survey type is a TOPO or "topographic" survey, which produces a large area map. This sort of map is much more intense, involves a lot more time and effort to acquire the needed data, takes a lot more work, and requires a survey team to be almost hyper-detailed.

When working to create a topographic survey, not only are landform variations and boundaries recorded, but changes in elevation on the given site are also recorded. This allows drafters to create maps showing significant land formations such as rivers, streams, valleys, caves, etc. The information provided on this type of map will also give the reviewer data on the lay of the land, such as whether the site has steep inclines or other general formations that, once recorded, allow anyone who wishes to make improvements to the place to be able to make informed decisions on what can or can't be built or what does or does not need to be improved on the site.

My team recently finished a series of small surveys for a land developer looking to design and build a few smaller gated residential communities in Central Florida. The data was given to our drafting team, who completed these drawings for our client.

That means our team was available and ready for the next project. Thus, I was called into the office on a Friday in late April to discuss a significant new project that had just come to the company.

As the chief surveyor on a team, I am responsible for meeting with management, getting the information provided by a prospective client, reviewing project details, and scheduling my crew to head to the site and begin work.

I met with management, and we reviewed the project. I felt stressed as we reviewed this project, which would be a TOPO map project. The project was located in a remote area of Southern Florida. We were forewarned that the site was wet most of the time. This area was not swampy, but it was damp and moist, and we were advised that you may not sink into swampy water when working on the site, but the site would appear "soggy" and wet.

As we reviewed documentation and client request information, I suddenly became aware that this would be a colossal project involving surveying the area for several miles in each direction. In addition, this would be a long-haul camping adventure that would require much work, be tiring, and keep our team away from home for as long as it takes to complete data collection.

One of the things I focused on most was how hot and humid it was going to be working on this project in May and potentially even going into June, depending again on the terrain and how long it would take us to collect all of the necessary coordinates for this map to be produced.

From experience, having grown up in these parts, I am fully aware that Central and Southern Florida can be brutal. With the moist environment, heat, and humidity, my team and I will likely spend most of the time wet, sweaty, and miserable. But, of course, this is just part of what you do when you are a land surveyor. You may be able to help collect data and allow for changes to an existing site, but you cannot change the climate or weather, so I was already expecting this to be a sticky job.

When a survey crew finishes a job at our company, team members are generally given a day or two to clean up their equipment, restock any needed supplies for the next project, and prepare to travel and camp out during the project. Again, some assignments could be minor and only require a day on-site, but a TOPO survey is much more detailed. Based on the scope I reviewed during our meeting, I determined, from experience, that this job would take a few weeks.

Management knew this would be tough with the climate, weather, and general wet terrain. Because they were already aware my team would be stationed on this job site for a few weeks, they had acquired two sizeable military-styled tents. Both tents were large. One would be large enough to allow all four of us to sleep in separate cots. The second tent would be our "office" space, including a portable desk and foldable shelving unit to store all our field equipment. At the end of each day, we would spend some time here to offload all of the data we had collected during the day. We would place this data into the computer system we used for all processes so the information would be safely stored and backed up by sending encrypted information to the home office. This allowed our drafting team to start configuring the drawing set of maps we would produce for this TOPO Survey.

The company provided all equipment and supplies, including a battery generator plugged into both tents to allow for power needs. We mainly needed this power supply to keep our data secure until we could get it back to the office for our drafting crew to translate, but there would be ample power for other things. The system also included solar panels so the batteries would replenish themselves. So again, it was an excellent system, and again, I was ecstatic that we now live in an age that has created such incredible technology.

We would, of course, also need power for lighting, and as I was reviewing the supply list, "Thank God," I saw a requisition for two, count 'em, "TWO" self-contained air conditioning units that would run off of the generator.

'*HOT DAMN*,' I thought. '*At least we won't sleep in our sweat at nighttime.*' I felt some of the stress I had been feeling suddenly reduced by quite a lot.

Since we would be in a remote location, we were also provided with food staples and were advised that additional supplies would be dropped to us as needed to relieve us from the requirement to travel to and from the site for those supplies.

I contacted my team. They were ready to get back out in the field and get to work. Sure, it is always nice to have a little break between projects, but after a day or two, most of us surveyors who were used to being out in the field were more than ready to get to it as we would begin to feel stir-crazy. We field survey guys are a unique breed. We can handle being inside an office but will start to feel closed in after a day behind a desk. We need to be out in the field, breathing the fresh air, feeling sunshine burning the back of our necks, and getting sweaty from a full day of hard work.

I advised the team of the project's scope and told them we would meet at the main office the following Monday, pack up all required equipment and supplies, which should take a couple of hours at best, and head to the job site. I had already calculated that we were looking at a 3 ½ -hour drive from the office to the new job site. Then I figured setting up camp would probably take 2 to 3 hours, including all equipment, tents, batteries, etc. So, Monday would be a "pack up, drive, and set up" day.

Everyone was on the same page and agreed we would meet first thing Monday morning at the main office and get moving on the next big project. Larger projects can be excellent, even though more work is involved because it gives the team working on the site a sense of stability. It's almost like you move into a tent, and you can actually "settle" down and feel most permanent, even if it's only for a few weeks. A few weeks on one job is often better than traveling to and from several projects and feeling like a migrant who is never settled.

As we wrapped up our video conference meeting, I advised the team to get plenty of rest and be ready to be wet, sticky, and sweaty for some time. I told them I trusted they wouldn't need to be advised of what types of clothing to pack for this "extended stay" experience. As usual, we would wear our company uniforms during working hours. This meant either khaki cargo shorts, the ones with all the pockets with flaps that allow you to carry a multitude of little things, or camel-colored long pants, again with lots of little pockets to help bring the little tools we need on-site, and knit collared button-down golf shirt with the company logo on the left chest.

When working in the field, you always want to ensure you are representing your company in case anything comes up that might present a liability or need an explanation from residents in the area. Believe it or not, many everyday citizens prefer to avoid interactions with land surveyors. Surveyors get a bad rap because, frequently, they are involved with establishing boundaries to allow for land improvements or even allow for land to be taken over by a local entity if it means bettering the overall community. You know, like widening a road and needing extra egress space via eminent domain. I've been on survey jobs where landowners would secretly follow us around and pull up the survey markers we have set to throw us off and make our jobs harder. It's not generally a huge issue because most of our documentation is digital. Still, it can be a nuisance if a land developer needs to be specific about the locations of property boundaries. Sometimes, you must return to the site and re-establish the important marker points if they have been illegally removed. This takes extra trip travel and time. So, again, it is best to show our company logo and name for our safety and protection and to present to the general public that we are working in their area on official business.

I advised the team to get to the store and stock up on bug spray and anything they thought they might want or need while we were away from civilization that was beyond the scope of supplies and equipment provided to us by the company because we would be on a very remote location in dense, damp, and swampy areas for most of our time on this project, there would be no quick runs to the store for anything forgotten. If you don't remember to pack it, you won't need it and can't get it once we have settled into our work encampment. We all laughed, sighed, and agreed we were looking forward to returning to the field, even if it sounded like it would not be the most pleasant of jobs.

I logged out of my system and started a checklist to remember everything on this trip. I pulled out sets of my typical survey uniform: cargo shorts, jeans or pants, work boots, heavy socks, t-shirts, and my button-front collared short-sleeve company "uniform." While packing my work shirts, I noted they were beginning to look a little tattered and threadbare. I usually try to wear my uniform shirts until they almost hang off of me before I requisition new ones. These shirts have been through the wringer and have served their purpose. I chuckled and jotted a note and left it on the counter at my place to remind me to order new shirts once we returned from this job. That relieved me because I thought, '*Ok, if I tear a shirt on some crazy scrub brush or something, it won't be the end of the world; it will just mean I'm stuck wearing a wrecked shirt until new ones can be ordered.*'

I always packed many bandanas. You could wrap one around your head to help keep the sweat under your hat from running into your face all day. And you can't forget about a hat, two or three. I know it's humid and moist down that way, but if the sun is out and you're roaming around in the swamp, you'll get burned quicker than sausage on a hot frying pan. Trust me; I've been there. Oh, and several pairs of underwear. I generally like to wear boxer briefs. They help me keep my BIG jewels packaged so they don't swing around and get damaged or damage anything else. They also seemed to help keep my junk from rubbing on my muscled thighs. This is handy in humid climates because less rubbing means less raw and irritated skin.

I guess to say I'm gifted down there would be an understatement. I have an 11" dick when I'm fully hard. It usually averages about 7" or 8" soft, and I'm not bragging about that. But, hey, don't laugh. And whatever you do, do NOT point. I'm already self-conscious of it as it is. I don't know where I got it because I never saw my dad's dick, nor my uncle's dick, so I had nothing to compare myself to. Our family was big on no nudity showing, which would even go as far as wearing long sleeves, longer shorts, or long skirts for the women folk. It wasn't religious; it was just that my folks were modest. And you would never be caught running around anywhere out in the public portions of the house without being clothed. I can hear my mom saying in her tinny voice, "Now, what the heck reason did you have to leave the bathroom with all God gave you swinging in the breeze just to run across the hall to your room? You didn't think someone might happen by?" Yeah, that kind of home environment.

So, the less "jangling" of my junk, no matter the situation, the better.

I guess I'm gifted or should be thankful in other ways. I lucked out and went through a growth spurt at about 15. I shot up from 5' 10" to 6' 4", which seemed to happen overnight. This added height certainly helped me in sports. I played basketball through most of high school and was pretty good. I was even good enough to be a team captain.

Unfortunately, basketball was not where my heart was, so it was a means to an end.

I received a scholarship to college and "played" my way to a bachelor's degree in land engineering, but again, basketball was just a tool. I didn't breathe and eat the sport; I just participated for camaraderie, health benefits, and a way to pay for more schooling. So, I guess you could say my heart wasn't really in it.

Having spent my formative years in sports meant I had learned early on that working out and keeping fit was crucial to several things in life. First, if you looked good, you felt good. If you looked good, others would find you good-looking. When I was younger, I noted that the more muscle I put on or, the tighter I could get my body to be, the luckier I got with the female species. I was never shocked but often surprised when I noticed some guys discreetly checking me out, just like the women. This didn't bother me unless they didn't take "No, I'm straight" for an answer. I never had any issues with anyone coming on too strong, but I was prepared to handle that situation if it arose. I also came across as intimidating because of my height and stature, so those who were unsavory or wanted to cause trouble generally steered clear of me.

One of my biggest problems was this giant piece of meat swinging between my legs. Girls I have dated would blush, and their eyes would go wide when they learned of my sizeable appendage, but as soon as they saw it, most of them crossed their legs, squeaked a frightened sigh, and ran away faster than an out-of-control steam locomotive.

Even though I played basketball, I was much thicker and carried more muscle than a typical basketball player. I have the height but had to work harder to glide across the floor during a game. This helped keep me in great shape, so I didn't mind the work it took.

Now, at 43, I can't complain about my body. As I said, I stand at 6'4". I have a 32" waist and a 48" chest. I lucked out and got the furry gene from my dad's side of the family. Although our family didn't condone nudity, on a few occasions, I'd go out to chop wood with Dad and my Uncle Ted, Dad's brother; they had no qualms about taking their shirts off while cutting wood and sweating. When they'd catch me staring and frowning at them, Dad was always the first to say, "What your mother doesn't know won't hurt any of us." He and Uncle Ted would slap each other on their sweaty backs, laugh at that comment, and continue chopping. I did catch enough glimpses of their muscled torsos and noted they were covered with thick, wavy hair from the base of their chins down to the top of their jeans, and it certainly looked like that hair traveled even further down.

So, I feel I wasn't too bad-looking. Tall, toned, thick from years of gym work, and furry from head to toe. I wish I could say the heavy 5 o'clock shadow on my face was the look I was going for, but it isn't. I shaved twice a day, and when in the office, sometimes it was three times. It seemed like just as soon as I walked out of the bathroom, I had that thick shadow again. I probably didn't help because I have always been interested in US Western History, especially cowboys and cowboy life. So, I am currently sporting a thick, long Fu-Manchu-type mustache and long sideburns. I know this may sound gay, but think of the biker guy from that musical group from the '70s, the Village something or other. He always wore leather and had that thick mustache. Well, anyway, I had come across some old tintype pictures of Wild West characters, and several guys were sporting that look, and I found it intriguing. So that's my current "mug," so to speak. I always joke to myself when I shower because if I let my beard grow out, which I have done in the past, it would get kinky and curly, and I think it would look like my public hair. They have the same color, texture, and even the same kinky curl to them when it's humid out. Unfortunately, my beard and pubes grow so thick that you almost can't run your fingers through them. Crazy, no?

I think the only place I don't have hair growing on my body is the tops of my feet and right behind my ears. I even have hair growing on my knuckles and toes. So, you can't say there's no primary testosterone pumping through my system. Although I was hairy pretty much all over, I also found it interesting that the hair around my nipples seemed to grow in a pattern as it circled my nipples. So, if you looked at my chest, you could see my pinkish brown puffy quarter-sized nipples glowing out of that chest hair. I was also self-conscious of this when I was younger because I thought people would think I trimmed my chest hair this way as some kinky fetish.

I will admit that my nipples are undoubtedly sensitive, and if you want to see me levitate off the bed, try playing with those thick buttons and see what happens. However, even though I have sensitive nipples, I do not shave or trim my chest hair to expose those nipples. I don't cut or shave anything, but maybe just a little on the back of my neck and under my chin where my neck and chest hair grow together. That spot can be distracting if you're sweaty and your hair rubs together whenever you move your head or breathe.

I have nicely defined thighs and arms from years of squats and curls. I like to run occasionally, but being outside a lot for work, I prefer a more regimented aerobics activity. So, I generally run on a treadmill in a little section of my place that I've set aside as a home gym. The cardio and lifting help keep my legs strong and thick and helps me keep that perky ass that so many men my age have already begun to let go flabby.

Let's say I've never had trouble with the ladies. So, whatever I'm doing must be working. But unfortunately, I never fell into that fad where you just had to have one or more tattoos. Sure, a tattoo is nice, but I never found it "nice" enough to spend the time and money or go through so much pain to inject my skin with ink. So, I am one of the misfits out there whose skin is a clean slate and shall remain clean at this stage in my life.

I may have a clean slate body, but I'm not neat. I drink and smoke with the best of them. I generally don't do hard drugs, but I am not afraid of booze, a cigar or cigarette here and there, and lots of weed.

I can only say, "Thank God this company doesn't drug test." I use marijuana to relax. I consider myself a responsible pot user. I finish my chores, and then it's time to kick back, smoke up, and let my mind take flight.

I spent the rest of the day Saturday finishing laundry, packing my travel bags, and slowly checking things off the list I had created.

Since this was a long-distance project, I knew we would be given two work trucks. The trucks would have all of the survey equipment and tools we would need to complete the task. Both vehicles would be crew cabs, so we'd have more space for storage, as two guys would generally drive in each truck. In addition, we had room to store luggage, food supplies, tents, and all accessories. It would be a fun trip but still require much work.

Sunday, as I packed things up, ensured my house was in order, and set my alarm, I sighed, "This will be a BIG project. So, here's to being tired but feeling accomplished when we are all done."

The last bag was packed. Dishes were done and put away, all perishable foods were eaten or thrown out, and everything was neat and ready to welcome me home once we completed this big job. I headed to bed.

Chapter Two

I generally don't sleep well when I know I have to be up at a particular time for a special reason, but I slept like a baby this time. I was shocked when the alarm went off on Monday morning because I had been sleeping so soundly. *'WOW,'* I thought, *'That's not like me, but I'll take it.'* I even felt rested this morning.

I felt good. I showered, woofed down a protein bar and some coffee, and rinsed everything so everything was clean and tidy. I rechecked my list, shut the door, set the alarm, and locked up.

I headed to my truck and drove to the office. I thought, *'Let's get this day going because it will be long.'*

I had advised my team to get to the office at 8:00 to double-check everything, ensure nothing was missing, and pack up and be on the road. Just like the dutiful assistant he is, Brent rolled into the back parking lot just as I was getting out of my truck. I raised my hand and waved, and I heard a little toot of his horn to acknowledge he had seen me. I started unpacking my equipment and supplies to transfer them to the company trucks. Brent parked, got out and proceeded to do the same thing.

I entered the office, and Trula was at the front desk. She's an attractive lady. I say "Lady" because she was an older woman past her prime but still thinks she is the cat's meow.

Don't get me wrong, she's as sweet as a coconut cream pie, but she can have the sour aftertaste of a diet key lime pie.

Anyway, I did my nice thing and wished her good morning. I saw that the BIG bosses weren't in yet, but they already knew what project my team and I were on, so there was no reason to report to anyone, and I was sure Trula would keep everyone informed. When I got to Trula's desk, she was smiling and had her hand out with two sets of truck keys for the two vehicles that had been requisitioned for us. I thanked her and hoped the rest of her week was great. She grinned, rolled her eyes, sipped her coffee, and said, "Yeah, thanks."

As I headed out to the trucks, Brent caught up. He had stacked all his stuff next to mine in the parking lot. I gave him one set of keys and told him he gets to be lucky and drive one of the two vehicles. Brent is a trooper. I never need to worry that he won't go along with whatever the procedure requires or whatever I ask him to do.

Brent and I have worked together long enough to learn much about each other. We may not be the type of guys who hang out on a Saturday night drinking beer and shouting at the game on TV, but we've shared enough life experiences that we sort of "know" one another. I guess like good friends, a brother, or maybe a cousin.

Brent is a pretty stout-looking guy. He stands at just about 6' 0," so I look down at him slightly, but that's cool because he is my assistant, so he should look up to me. Brent has a thin beard that comes forward on his face and turns into a mustache and goatee. He keeps everything trimmed close to his face, so you know he has a beard, but it's pretty sleek or slick. He does trim the beard into a thinner strip along his chin; they call that a "chin-strap" nowadays. But no matter how much he trims or shaves, he has the same issues I have with a constant amount of scruffy and angry whiskers that seem to grow with every breath he takes. So, there's a shadow where his natural beard grows, and then lower on his chin, you see the beard hairs that have been allowed to grow longer. I'd say Brent probably trims at least every 2 or 3 days. Unfortunately, I don't have time for that. It's bad enough that I must be careful not to accidentally trim off one or both sides of my mustache when I quickly whip through my trimming and shaving regimen and am usually half asleep.

Brent is all muscle. A while ago, he was on a ladder, and I was holding it for stability, and the tag on his Levi's read 33" x 36". I'd say he's probably got a 42 or 44-inch chest, so he's got a pretty stout taper from his chest to his waist. He tends to enhance that by generally wearing that same uniform type khaki button-down long or short-sleeved shirt; sometimes he will have a t-shirt or muscle shirt underneath, but most of the time, he wears the shirts, and they are usually unbuttoned at least 2 or 3 buttons from the top. With his muscled chest, his pecs and shoulders pull at the fabric of his shirts and cause them to pull apart at the buttons. Brent has a very thick swirl of chestnut fur that covers his pecs. On a sweltering day, when he's got his shirt opened for ventilation and he's sweating, you can see the shiny place between the mountains we will call his pecs as the sweat runs from his neck down the top of his pecs and trickles down that furry crevasse on the way to his abs, or at least I presume. I've honestly never seen Brent out of his regular work attire. And he wears that same attire whether at work, a party, or doing some company event, so I've never seen him in anything else.

Brent usually wears Levi's. He must only own 2 or 3 pairs of jeans, or at least the ones he wears while working, but they are almost threadbare. There have been recent jobs where I've caught my breath thinking if he bent over one more time, the thin area at the bottom of his jeans would split, and we would all be slapped in the face when the explosion occurred. On miserably hot and sticky jobs, he has been known to follow the rest of us and wear his khaki cargo shorts so at least his legs can breathe.

Anyway, Brent has a good look. He has hazel eyes but is usually always wearing his work-type sunglasses. Heck, I wouldn't be shocked if he wore them indoors at night while watching TV. Sometimes, I've jokingly wondered if his glasses were riveted to his head like an old action figure.

He had recently split from his girlfriend of 5 years. Trust me; I met that bitch affectionately known as his girlfriend at one of our company functions. It was all I could do not to pull Brent aside and start telling him about the Birds and the Bees, more importantly about that part about men who are pussy-whipped and who need to put down the law. But you know how friends can be. We don't want to be the harbinger of bad news, so we patiently wait and watch things crumble. But we are always there as a shoulder to cry on, and that's when we tend to say, "Well, you know, now that we think about it, that person did show some red flags, etc." Trust me, this "friends" thing is something that has gone on since time eternal.

Anyway, Brent and I had shared a few beers over this breakup, and he was coping, but he was still fighting some demons. So, I hoped being "off-grid" on this significant project might help him clear his mind and be ready for the next great adventure.

All of that said, Brent was a mule. On top of the bulked chest, shoulders, and rock-solid abs, he sported some amazing pistons the rest of us would call legs. He had been a running back in college, and that's how he and I connected. In addition, we both discovered a love for college football.

So, again, we didn't hook up like two high school girls every night, but we would occasionally get together and shoot the shit. I could count on Brent to carry, pack, pick up, or toss anything that needed to be dealt with.

This would be useful because frequently, you are in the middle of nowhere when doing a TOPO survey. So, sometimes, you will have to yank out your trusty machete and hack through the scrub and growth; to find that shot, you need to help finish collecting the coordinates required to plot the site. So, I had faith that Brent would be the guy to chop the shit out of anything and everything that came across his path. And I knew I was going to need this brazen strength.

Although the guys and I have worked together as a team for some time, this will be the most critical survey job they have ever worked on. I've been on some massive projects, but to my knowledge, this will be the first large and long job the other three on my team will have experienced. This would be challenging, but I was sure it would be fun and a learning experience for everyone.

I saw Roger roll in as Brent and I unlocked and opened the two trucks. He was still on time, but dammit, he was cutting it close, just like he always did. As his vehicle pulled closer to us, I noticed two heads in the cab. The sun showed brightly into the cab, and I saw Cliff riding with Roger. So, I thought, *'At least both are here and on time.'*

They pulled up, driving too fast and stirring dust in the parking lot. Then, after the dusty haze settled, they got out of Roger's truck, each pulling a medium-sized backpack over their shoulder while heading to where Brent and I were loading the field trucks.

I said, "Hey, welcome, gentlemen. Are you ready for a BIG adventure?" We all laughed heartily. As I glanced at Roger and Cliff, I asked, "That's all you're bringing with you? You realize we may be in the field for a few weeks."

They both grinned, held up their cell phones, tablets, and headphones, nodded, and said, "YEP, we travel lightly; what's the point of bringing four pairs of underwear when one will work for several days." They acknowledged we were all men, and men stink when hot and working, so we'd all better get used to the stink and get on with this job. I liked their carefree attitude, but this wasn't a free ticket to being overly filthy or unclean. Everything has limits. We all agreed and laughed again.

All I could think was how little those two young guys were bringing along for this long project. Finally, I chuckled and thought, '*Well, there's only one way to learn, and that's to do. Right? And if they believe they will sap all of our battery power to charge up their devices daily, I will put them both on bicycles wired to the generator and make them pedal for their pleasure.*'

I rolled my eyes and thought, '*Young kids these days.*'

We four opened the storage doors behind the office. Two large piles were neatly stacked with the camping and surveying equipment needed for this large project. We looked at one another, and I told everyone what to pick up and where to pack it.

I noted Roger and Cliff more closely as we worked to make some order out of the chaos. Lately, we've been so busy that we all met each morning, climbed into our trucks, and headed to whatever site we were scheduled to survey. Then, we would work all day, drive back to the office, and mumble to one another as we sauntered to our vehicles and went to our prospective homes.

As we loaded the trucks, I noted that Roger had filled out quite a bit over the past few months. His standard uniform attire looked tight, almost as if he was close to busting seams here and there. I thought, '*Looks like someone else needs to put in a requisition for new uniforms once we get back from this project.*' I made myself a mental note to advise Roger once we returned.

I remembered Roger talking about some new workout routines he had been following, so maybe I hadn't noticed this significant change because we were now coming out of the winter months, and although many land surveys had to be placed on hold due to inclement weather, some field work still could be performed. So, we would see each other daily while on our team, but everyone would be bundled in coats and hoodies, hats, masks, and gloves. I grinned and thought, "I guess this is the first time I've seen Roger "less dressed" in quite some time.

And, even though this is Florida, we can still have some pretty chilly weather. And if you live in a warmer climate for any length of time, I jokingly say your blood thins, so even 50 degrees on a sunny day can seem chilly to us thin-blooded long-term residents.

I passed Roger on one of our many trips to and from the pile and trucks and said, "Man, you been workin' out? You're all bulked up."

Roger grinned, lowered his head a little, and then said, "Yeah, my girlfriend couldn't stop talking about all of the hunks we saw when we were down in Miami last fall, so I started working out with the thought that it's good for my health, but also good for me in the bedroom." I laughed, and he chuckled nervously, and we continued shuffling equipment.

Whatever Roger was doing was paying off. Roger was already a lucky guy because he, too, had played sports in high school and college. Roger was fortunate to have that typical "jock" type of body. You know, broad shoulders, meaty pecs, thick arms, tapering to a narrow but tight and muscular waist, then moving down to tight jeans that always looked like they would pop, and rivets would start flying around like bullets. I don't know how Roger could be comfortable when it looked like his hard bulging ass and his thick bulging crotch were both stuffed into his jeans. Of course, we guys don't talk about that, but that doesn't mean we don't wonder about it. Don't get me wrong, they looked good on him and accentuated his manly assets, so I'm sure he was enjoying all of the female attention he could get from this hard work. Roger was also one of those rare ginger-haired guys. I've seen these guys before. They tend to have pale skin, but it's not pasty and has a reddish swarthiness. That breed of ginger man tends to be able to stick his finger in his mouth, blow, and puff up his muscles like Popeye does when he eats spinach. I was jealous of those guys when I was in school because they could stand around the gym, joking and laughing, do a couple of sets of this or that movement, and the next day, they'd be strutting in the locker room all pumped and chiseled and here I had to work and work at it to maintain my buffed appearance.

Roger had developed muscles on top of muscles but was a lean, mean fighting machine to use an old cliché. Roger's entire body was covered in a fine layer of ginger hair. You almost couldn't see it unless you caught him at a certain angle in the sunlight, and then you could see the sun causing the hairs on his body to glisten and glow as he worked and sweated. Roger wore jeans or cargo shorts and tight-fitting t-shirts that hugged his torso like a glove.

Roger has a short but thick ginger beard and mustache. Being 25, Roger still has what we older guys might call "peach fuzz" here and there. He has a thick head of hair that he keeps buzzed in a military-style, high-n-tight. A few places on his cheeks, chest, and shoulders are covered in ginger freckles. I have never been a fan of people with freckles, but they looked good in all the right places on Roger. Lucky kid.

Cliff was a "pot-stirrer" or "prankster" if ever there was one. At 19, this was his first job. His dad knew someone who knew someone in upper management, and Cliff needed a job to earn some cash before he went away to college in the fall. Cliff's dad had decided it was a good idea for Cliff to sit out a year between high school and college and get a real job, earn money, and be a real man for a little while. On the other hand, Cliff wanted to be young, carefree, and party before he was too old to do anything fun. Cliff had played baseball in high school and was pretty good as a shortstop. Unfortunately, he had gotten into trouble with booze, and when he was caught with a joint in his car, even his dad's "friends in high places" couldn't help him beat that rap. That was the end of Cliff's short baseball career.

Luckily, Cliff escaped total ruination by not going to jail. After all, Dad could help a little, but Cliff had been reprimanded to his dad's custody on good behavior. Let's say Cliff felt he was now living in a concentration camp. So, he went to work, came home, ate, played games, went to bed, and got up the following day, and it was the same, day in and day out.

Cliff's mom had passed away from a short illness a couple of years ago, which drove Cliff's dad into overkill mode. Nevertheless, he did everything he could to push Cliff to succeed and considered Cliff precious material since he was the only thing remotely close to his wife, so he needed to be protected at all costs. Unfortunately, Cliff seemed to buck every rule or instruction he got from his dad. Dad just couldn't let Cliff grow up in his own time and in his own way.

So, Cliff was a prankster. He needed to get attention because he seemed to recede into the woodwork when home, well, unless he had done something else wrong again. This is why Cliff was always cracking jokes, making some annoying sound, or slapping one of us, or you name it. For the most part, we all allowed it and snickered and would mutter, "Youth." I was a little worried that being out here in the middle of nowhere with minimal contact with the outside world, I might end up dealing with a complete basket case and watch Cliff start running around like a deranged Robbie the Robot, with his head about to explode from lack of outside distractions.

'*Oh well,*' I thought, '*if that happens, I'm just going to throw Cliff off a cliff and hand him over to Brent to put him back together again.*' Again, I laughed and thought, '*Thank God for Brent.*'

Everyone pitched in, and in less than my predicted two-hour timeframe, we loaded the survey field trucks. We checked and rechecked our lists. Everything was in place. Everything was secure, and it was time to get behind the wheel and head to the job site.

I would lead our little caravan and decided to take Roger with me in my truck and let Brent enjoy Cliff's company. I don't dislike Cliff; please don't get me wrong. But Cliff is that young, arrogant guy who thinks he's God's gift to anything and everything. You know the type; he's just a young cocky guy who hasn't been bitch-slapped and made aware that he has a place in this great world we all live in, just like the rest of us. And that place is fixed, so sooner or later, someone will knock him down to his proper notch in life, and he'll succeed where he's meant to be. Until then, I had trouble dealing with that attitude." Cliff's pranks, like frequently squirting one of us with water on a hot day or farting while we were in the truck heading to or from a job and then laughing about it for miles as we rolled down windows and gagged, were tolerable, but they did annoy me, and I tried very hard to stay calm about it. On the job, I may be his boss, but I was not his dad, so I didn't feel I had the right to punish him unless he got out of control. We would all generally get a laugh out of these things, but after a couple of chuckles, I was usually over all those childish games and would focus on the job at hand and try to ignore Cliff's antics.

So, I decided to take the easy way out, stick Cliff with Brent, and have Roger tag along with me. Roger was a good kid. Although he was 25, he wasn't as wet behind the ears as Cliff was at 19; I could still detect some immaturity in Roger. The difference between Roger and Cliff was that Roger would step back and think about things when called out and try to change his actions or procedures based on his input. Cliff was just a bull in a China shop and didn't like being told what to do. If I'm lucky, I hope I can help Cliff grow and see that he will get further in life if he plays the game instead of bucking it or thinking he can change the outcome because he thinks he's "somebody." But, again, I feel that parenting skills are not part of my job description.

Cliff is a tight little bulldog of a man. He stands at about 5' 9". I often wonder if he is a scrapper because he feels he needs to compensate for his lack of size by having a more dominant personality. Cliff will wear the company-prescribed cargo shorts but generally wears tight-fitting blue jeans, ripped here and there, and usually looks like they are way past laundry time or have missed it altogether. He has that musky, manly smell, but it isn't terrible, even though you'd think otherwise based on how "gunky" his jeans look. He has a severe masculine face. His jaw juts proudly and forms sharp corners where it meets his chin.

Cliff is still in the process of "trying" to grow a full beard. His scruffy face is made more noticeable because his beard grows very patchy. He's one of those guys with dark hair, but if out in the sun often, his hair will take on a reddish tint and almost turn blond in places. Cliff always wears a ballcap. He likes to wear his cap tipped back on his head, and it looks like he has spent hours cupping and shaping the brim of his hats to be curved just right. Cliff has that gruff redneck stud look about him with that cocky way of wearing his hats. I don't think I've ever seen him out of his ball cap. I've jokingly thought he probably sleeps with his ballcap on at night.

Cliff has a tight body. He has a broad chest that tapers to a narrow waist, but he has just a bit of a gut, probably from all the beer he drinks. However, he still has a hot look about him because he generally wears a large cowboy belt buckle. It is a championship belt from some bull riding competition he tried when he was younger. He typically leaves the tails of his work shirt hanging outside his jeans and only tucks the front portion of his t-shirt into his pants behind the belt buckle. This tends to accentuate the buckle and the bulge in his jeans just below that and also camouflages the beer gut just enough so you wouldn't know it's there.

We were ready to head out.

We said our goodbyes to those who had arrived at the office, of which there were very few that early in the morning. Most arrived around 9:00 in the morning, but on Mondays, people were a little more relaxed about getting to work. Management didn't mind because that was one of the beauties of this company, that they understood and respected flextime. As long as the work was done and completed on time and budgets and profits were kept intact, there was no need to treat everyone like some paid servant. Trula assured us she would tell the BIG WIGS that we had checked in and were on the road. So, we ensured our radios and equipment were all charged, climbed into our assigned trucks, and began our journey.

For the next few weeks, our only communications with the office would be via remote satellite transmissions, and we could get cell signals here and there, but I was not holding my breath that this would feel like some high-tech resort. So, with the project's remoteness, it may feel like working and walking on the moon. OK, it's not that bad, but I cannot stress the remoteness of this job site.

Even though I feared the worst when it came to the young guys on the team trying to deal with no cell signal, I also grinned because I could not wait to hear them screaming and crying. After all, they couldn't check their emails or watch videos on their devices without a signal. This would be a rude awakening for the youngsters, taking them out of their typical "digital" environment. Sure, we were all outdoorsmen and enjoyed camping, hiking, fishing, and those types of activities, but that would tend to be a weekend event, and young people can generally go for a couple of days without cell service. After a few days, most of today's "kids" will start showing signs of internet and text withdrawals. So even though this was going to be sort of like a camping trip, this was going to be a weeks-long event potentially. There will be a big difference, requiring some "mature" adjustments for everyone.

I had already input the coordinates for our camp into the GPS NAV for each vehicle but figured Brent would do what he usually does and follow me. I was right. At about 3 ½ hours, we pulled up to a gravel drive that had seen better days. There was an old iron gate across the passage. I had been given instructions in my information packet, so I knew the procedure for opening the gate and pulling through so we could make our trek back to the best place to set up camp.

The going was slow. This road had been an access road many years ago, but it didn't appear to have been used much recently. Our vehicles had 4x4 capabilities, so I wasn't worried, but after driving for a solid 3 hours, I knew we were all getting mentally tired and still had to set up camp before nightfall.

We slowly made our way deeper into the property. We had old maps and survey information that our research team had put together for us, so it wasn't like we were driving blind, but it was still slow going.

Suddenly, just about where I thought we should be seeing it, I noticed a clearing. A large slab of limestone formed a floor in the clearing. The rest of the area did look wet. We had been lucky and had not run into muddy areas while driving back to the place that would become our home base. Still, moss was hanging in the trees; the sky had that white color to it, like it was so steamy the blue color of the sky was being blocked out, and everything seemed to take on a creepy appearance.

I stopped my truck, and Brent pulled up alongside me, rolling his eyes. I rolled down the passenger window, heard Cliff rattling on about something, and immediately knew why Brent's eyes were "rolling." Roger looked over at me, grinning, and I grinned sheepishly in Brent's direction and got a frosty "YOU OWE ME" look. '*OK*,' I told myself, '*I'll worry about that later.*' I looked at my old map and yelled that we were where we needed to be. Brent acknowledged, and we circled our trucks to form an old settlers' camp using our trucks as a solid backdrop or base for the center.

Once parked, everyone poured out and took off in different directions. It was time for everyone to piss off their morning coffee; riding in a truck for several hours and having one's kidneys banged left and right made the need to piss much more intense.

I got back to the truck first and started pulling out the tents and setting up equipment. Cliff came out of the woods and helped me lay the tent bases. He asked if I had ever been on a large project like this before, and I said I had and this was going to be much work and require much focus, at least during the day while we were out taking measurements. Cliff just grinned and nodded as we continued putting the tents together.

When Cliff and I pulled the lift cables on the first tent, Roger and Brent came out of the woods and started working on the second tent. Within an hour, we had both tents up and battened down. I couldn't get over how the look of these old off-white canvas tents reminded me of those old black and white photos of Civil War encampments full of this same type of military tent. I recall seeing images of this type of military-style tent from old Civil War documents I'd researched just for fun. Don't get me wrong, I love camping, but it's much more fun to camp in a tent where you can stretch out. I've done the whole two-person or four-person tent, which is different and can frequently feel cramped and unpleasant. These tents were almost like soft-walled cabins. You could stand up and walk around just like being in a house. So, I thought, '*Heck. Throw in a fireplace and a nice recliner; I could call it home.*'

Most of our foodstuffs were easy, quick meals, like the military. But, again, it takes a particular type of guy to be comfortable doing this kind of work. It demands a lot out of a person, and you have to be able to adapt quickly. So, we wouldn't be doing much heavy cooking, but we did have a small camp stove and set up an area where we could have a small contained campfire later.

I was surprised but forever thankful that the office had supplied us with a camp-styled shower kit, which consisted of a large plastic bag that could be hung high in a tree or off the tent. As long as you had enough elevation, you would boil water or collect fresh spring water…. it would heat in the sun and provide us with a shower. It wasn't strong, but it could help get some of the daily grime off us. The last thing we want is to get some jungle rot or something. If anyone asks, YES, I have gotten a rash in a place like this, so I would be hyper-aware of our condition.

By late afternoon on Monday, we had both tents set. We had our campfire pit dug and set up. We had chairs, a place for the camp stove, trash, and other items we needed. I was impressed with whoever had specified the tents, as the sleeping tent was set up, so it was divided into four sections, almost like four rooms. Granted, there was still only one entrance to the tent, but once inside, you walked through one room, and each room had a small opening covered with a flap for privacy. So, you could easily sleep four people in this tent without anyone getting on top of anyone else. A minor issue is that if you were sleeping in the room with the main entrance, everyone else would have to pass you to get in and out of the tent. Those late-night piss runs would be annoying if someone in that space weren't a heavy sleeper. This would be useful during our extended stay and allow everyone some personal space to retreat when needed.

Thank God for the limestone slab. We felt it best to set up the tents on that slab to keep any excess moisture from wicking into them. We could rig tie-downs and cabling so the tents were secure and stabilized. The only thing they would not survive would be a hurricane, and, to my knowledge, no storms were predicted this early in the season. We planted a couple of citronella torches to help keep the bugs at bay. I was surprised there weren't as many bugs annoying us as I had thought. But, again, I'm not complaining. Anytime you complain about not having as many bugs as expected, it is a good time in Florida.

Now that we had camp set up, it was nearing time to think about fixing something to eat and then just trying to chill out and relax because the "real" work begins bright and early tomorrow morning. Because our team has worked together for some time, we've been on a few overnighters, but never something this big. However, being the "family" we were, we had already gotten through the growing pains that new groups go through when they learn about one another over time. On one of these "overnighters," we all discovered we loved weed. Booze was okay, but it wasn't as unique as weed. We had all shared a while back that we hated the hangover you'd get from drinking alcohol but didn't have that type of issue with pot.

With the battery generator humming in the background, we set up the A/C units, the shower, charging stations, and desks. We even had a small battery-operated refrigerator to keep some perishables. Again, thank God for the new technology. I've been on rough surveys, but I can't imagine doing it as they did back in the 1800s.

We had our chairs arranged around the fire pit. The group decided to make sandwiches and eat something a little lighter. I noted that everyone was sweaty and looked wet, as if we had just walked through a shower and it had dumped water over most of our bodies. As we threw together some sandwiches with cold cuts, cheese, and bread, Brent cracked open a bottle of whiskey, and we each grabbed a cold beer out of the cooler. We ate, drank, and swatted bugs away from us. The citronella candles were helping, but you know what I've already said, "Florida bugs are just insane."

As the sun set, we cleaned up our dinner mess. Then, I asked Roger and Cliff to run out around our site and collect as much scrap wood as they could find so we could set up a fire. Even though it was hot and humid, I knew from experience that the dampness could feel cold to the skin once the sun finally went down. So, I wanted that fire going to help take the edge off.

The boys returned with armloads of small limbs and twigs, and we set out to build our first campfire. Again, camping nowadays is a breeze. We had a roaring fire in our fire pit within minutes and just in time. A chilling mist rolled into our area as the sun finally dived into the horizon. With dusk shining eerily through the moss-covered trees and shimmering as the fog ebbed and flowed, I got chilled and scooted my chair closer to the fire. The mist was funny because it had an eerie greenish tint to it. I had not seen this before in all my years as a Florida native, so I figured it must be just a combination of swamp gas, grasses, and humid conditions. However, the mist did have a subtle salty-sweet smell. I didn't say anything, but to me, it smelled like dried cum. It had that musky smell I'd smelled in my shorts once or twice.

I shook my head and thought, '*Naw, I must be tired, and my mind is making things up now.*'

I decided now was the time to light up a joint and get settled. As soon as I pulled out the joint and lit up, I had hands and eyes all over me, waiting for me to "puff, puff, pass." Instead, I looked at everyone, exhaled a thick funnel of smoke, laughed, and handed the doobie to Brent. I kept thinking, '*Like Pavlov's dogs, we all have one or more things we cannot pass up.*'

We were near the fire, gazing into the flames, only breaking our concentration whenever the joint or bottle of whiskey passed by. In my mind, I thought, '*This was the ideal way for a "family" to act.*' I have often wondered if the office knows what we go through in the field like this. Do they know we must let loose so we don't lose our minds when we start this intense work? I inhaled deeply, took a swig from my cup, and exhaled.

All is great with the world, and I already knew the pot and alcohol would help me sleep like a baby.

As the campfire began to dwindle, I could hear crickets and frogs start calling and would occasionally hear the subtle hoot of an owl somewhere off in the distance. On top of the food, booze, and pot, all this was relaxing me, and I was beginning to nod off. I noticed the other three guys were quiet as well. We were all contemplating the big day tomorrow.

We talked off and on about the project. I filled them in on the vast amount of land we would be surveying and how this would be the most significant project any of them had experienced up to this point in their careers. I advised the team that this parcel of land was not square with the world, and there were many bends and setbacks, so it would take longer to complete this work than on a typical square lot. We would be at the mercy of the data we collected, and that man-collected data could contain man-made errors, so we had to be always alert.

I glanced at my watch and noted it was about 9:00. Darkness had set in, and I finally said, "Enough shop talk for one night."

Everyone agreed.

I took a stick and stirred the embers and ashes that still smoldered. I told the guys I was about ready to hit the bed and get some rest so I was prepared for tomorrow. The guys agreed. We simultaneously jumped up, someone tossed some water on the fire to ensure it was out, and we grabbed our lantern and headed into the sleeping tent.

Off in the distance, I heard two loons calling back and forth. Man, this was relaxing, even if I was still wet and sweating.

Chapter Three

As the guys and I slept in our tent, little did we know what was going on about 4 miles down the road from us, at least as the crow flies. It is more like 6 miles when hiking through the brush.

Anyway…

Along the same main road, my team had driven down to get to the parcel we would be surveying, way off the road and up a slight incline, deep in the swampy woods, you could make out what looked like a small flame. Looking more closely, you could see an array of tanks, collection buckets, spigots, and various tubes and canisters. This was a moonshine still. As the flame flickered, it was heating a pressure tank. There were jets of steam shooting here and there. There was a slight hissing sound permeating this little clearing.

Pete Warnock, a local guy whose family had settled in this area centuries ago, had inherited the extensive and secluded parcel of land nearby from his dad. He was sitting shirtless and smoking a cigarette. He was squatted down, listening to the hissing of his prized possession. Pete had learned how to make this brew from his father, who had learned it from Pete's grandfather, and so on. Pete sat as the sun descended and drew little pictures in the dirt. Then, shadows grew while sucking on his cigarette, and everything took on an eerie glow.

Pete sat there, coping with the humidity, heat, and damp climate. He had lived in this his entire life, so it wasn't anything new. He used to joke and tell people he respected the heat and humidity, and when it got sweltering and humid, the best thing to do was to sit still, breathe calmly, and try to stay calm. So that's exactly what he was doing right now.

Pete's family, astoundingly, had run a still on this property for generations, and no one had ever been caught or had any "run-ins" with the law. Sure, there have been some close calls. Still, for the most part, the Warnock family has kept to themselves and generally kept a low profile in the small towns surrounding the area. For the most part, they are just another small-town family. However, having their name connected to a famous and delectable "spirit water" that has been and still is sought out for miles around might make them more prominent than they want to be.

He was bringing his latest "cook" up to temperature. From experience, Pete knew it took a couple of hours to get up to cooking heat and then another hour to cook the mash down to get the required "proof" he was looking for. His specialty was cooking the liquid at lower temperatures for more extended periods. This created an even stronger alcoholic content and helped keep open heating/cooking fires from being "noticed" in the wilderness. He was excited about this latest "cook" because a good friend, a girl named Dawn, had given him a boatload of discarded grains.

Dawn is a "nice" girl with whom Pete occasionally fucks; no beating about the bush on that one. He fucks her more for gain than sexual pleasure, but sex is sex, right? And she sure seems to get off whenever he shoves his throbbing dick into her somewhat loose vagina, so what's fair is fair, and they both generally get something out of their "connection."

Dawn works as a technician at the large scientific outpost, where they create and study new virulent forms of common grains to help produce more robust grains to help fight food shortages worldwide. The Team's current experiments are devoted to developing strains of grain that grow more quickly, are immune to most pests, cook down more quickly, and create an even higher proof of alcohol. Of course, this research is for making legitimate alcoholic beverages and fuels, not the illegal type like Pete cooks. But what the authorities didn't know wouldn't hurt them.

Dawn would let Pete know when they were tossing a new strain of grains, often asking if he would like to use it and see if he could make something of it. Of course, Pete always jumped at the chance to use a new product, but it also helped him stay off the grid by not having to find ways to purchase many grains for his still. And Dawn wasn't the hottest chick around, but he could get it up now and then and get her rocks off if it kept her on his good side and kept her supplying him with the much-needed natural products for his "business" needs. The way Dawn wailed the last time they "hooked up," Pete was sure she enjoyed meeting him and giving him some leftover grains because he'd given her a pork or two. You know, keeping it all down on the farm.

What Pete was unaware of was that this time, when Dawn called, she was onto him and had learned that he tended only to show attention and fuck her whenever he needed a new batch of something to cook in that damned old still of his. She was furious. You know that adage, "A woman scorned." And here she thought he liked her. Pete had never given her any indication of his undying love for her, but she always felt so special whenever she spent time with him. She had hoped there might be a future with him. But she had heard from some of her closest female friends that Pete was recently seen at a few swimming BBQ events, with a sleazy chick on each knee and kissing a third who was rubbing the other two women's tits. It was indeed a spectacle. Pete was so drunk that he wasn't aware that others had seen this offensive performance.

To get revenge on Pete this time, Dawn gave him an even more "special" load of grain. This grain had been through radiation but was infused with estrogen and testosterone.

The results were inconclusive, so the waste product was another failed experiment. No one knew what sort of side effects could occur from this strange mix, so it was deemed it would be destroyed.

Fuming as she smirked and leered, Dawn gladly handed over this grain to a smiling Pete and got the ritualistic kiss-on-the-cheek response. As Pete pulled back, he said, "Hey, maybe we can get together soon for a little fun."

Dawn squinted and nodded while grinning as she thought, '*Yes, sure if you live to see another day after you cook this stuff.*'

Pete was oblivious, grinned, and waltzed out of the lab with his prize hidden in a fake labeled delivery transport box.

So, Pete sat there, listening to the crickets start chirping and hearing the occasional frog burp here and there. Pete loved living out here in the remote swamp area. He wasn't a "people" person, so living remotely was okay. However, he did live with his brother, Marcus. But Marcus was family; after all, he'd been forced to "put up" with him since he came out of their mother's womb.

Pete had taken care of Marcus for years. When Pete was 20, Marcus was 16, and both of their parents were trapped in the swamp during a terrible storm and drowned. It was tragic, and it took Pete and his little brother quite some time to recover slowly from the loss. Because Pete was almost an adult of legal age, he was allowed to keep Marcus with him, and they lived in the house where both had been born and had grown up. They had inherited some money and the property where they were born. They didn't need much more than that.

Pete had just turned 24 but had begun to make some money by selling his "shine" to friends and family when he was only 22. Because the recipe had been around for quite some time, his family's recipe and reputation preceded it. Pete didn't even have to market his product much. Word of mouth did wonders.

The only thing Pete had to worry about was the Sheriff. But, again, due to the remoteness of this area, Pete was a little less concerned about running into the "bogeyman." He had been "cooking" at this current location for a year or more. He figured since this entire area was swamp-like, an old family farm, and would be hard to build on, there should be no reason to worry that someone would come along and discover his "factory," so to speak. So, this was one less worry for Pete.

Even with this built-in comfort, Pete has been known to pick up the entire kit and move it to various other locations on his property. And after a great year of "cooking" here, he thought it was about time for him to consider a move. He firmly believes it's always harder to locate and hit a target if it's frequently moving.

Pete had grown up in a strict household. His dad was retired from the military, and they lived by the military creed of authority and discipline. So, when his parents died, Pete and Marcus went wild for a bit. They both partied, fucked chicks, drank, smoked, and probably did everything possible to break the law without getting into trouble.

After a couple of years of this craziness, they both had settled down a little more and realized that all parties all of the time were not the best way to live a life. So, Pete decided Marcus should go to college, and he was there to work hard to help make his kid brother's life something more than the life he, himself, lived.

Pete worked, but he was mainly a handyman. He was a jack of all trades, so he could repair anything brought to him, and, again, he had garnered a reputation for being a mechanical wizard. With his handyman income and the money he brought in for selling his "shine," Pete was doing OK.

Pete had been a shy boy in school. Yes, he graduated from high school but made average to less-than-average grades and didn't consider himself clever enough to think about college. On the other hand, he had an inquisitive mind and didn't see the benefit of spending much money on education when he was more content to have a job paying the bills and more free time to do the things he felt were more fun.

He wasn't into sports, art, music, or anything the rest of his class found interesting. So instead, he spent most of his free time either working with his father, tearing down old buildings and selling the scrap materials, or working out at the gym because he genuinely enjoyed the pump and sweat he got from those workouts.

Pete's focus, devotion to the gym, and hard work shared with his father had turned him into a jacked-up muscleman. Pete had a swarthy complexion, and that swarthiness was enhanced by the fact that Pete was covered in dark fur. He had taken his shirt off because of the humidity. As he squatted near the still, the heat from the fire and the moisture caused his entire body to glisten in the evening light. Sweat was dripping off his scruffy chin, dripping onto his chest, running between his furry pecs, and trickling down his stomach and to his jeans, slowly but surely starting to dampen and soak all around his waist. But, again, this was normal for Pete. He just tolerated it by not moving much. The less energy you expended on a hot, humid day like today, the better off you were, especially if the simple act of breathing was enough to bring on a sweat.

Pete kept his hair cut short in a military-type fashion. Less mess to worry about. He had deep-set dark eyes covered with a thick brow ridge. He had sharp, manly facial features. When he was younger, the girls he dated often told him he should become a model. He usually just laughed and rolled his eyes when he'd hear this. He had thick facial hair that he tried to trim and shave to look neat. You didn't want to scare the little homemakers who called you to fix a broken light switch or door lock and show up looking like an ape. Unfortunately, no matter how hard he tried to keep his face looking "pleasant," he could not keep up with the facial scruff. His thick mustache covered his upper lip entirely. It protruded to the point where it almost looked like an overhanging ridge in a mountain, covering the opening to a secret cave. Pete could often be caught running his fingers through his mustache to help keep the hairs out of his mouth.

As the crickets and frogs' song grew louder and dusk slowly started to turn to darkness, Pete took one final draw on his cigarette, threw the butt under the fire cooking his prized product, stood up, rubbed his torso from his chest to his waist and shook the extra sweat off of his hands.

As he stood there looking at the still as it cooked away, he suddenly heard that telltale sound when liquid hits a flame. You know, like something sizzling that shouldn't be sizzling. Pete knew his moonshine still well enough that any strange or different sound would alert him immediately that something was amiss. He was well aware that anything out of the ordinary that wasn't part of his routine could cause attention to be drawn to the area, and Pete was sure he did not want to rouse any attention.

Pete had perfected the venting system on his still, consisting of a network of leftover ductwork he had scavenged from various building worksites and painted black and camouflaged using paint from old cans he had lying around from various handyman projects. He was proud of this "fancy work," as he jokingly called it. The system worked well enough that he could have a fire going to cook his precious product, but smoke and off-gases were kept to a minimum. His little ductwork setup would cause the smoke and gases to break down so rapidly that they would return to the atmosphere as heat or steam. The levels of gases, smoke, and heat were so low that you'd have to be on the still before noticing anything in the air.

The area where Pete's still is currently located is not on his property but on what would be considered a public easement between the neighboring property and his family's property. Pete felt it his right to use this small forgotten parcel of land for his operation because, after all, the land was stolen from his family when it was deemed the easement was necessary for public health issues. The family had been paid a healthy sum, but they never felt it was enough and felt the local or federal government was still overstepping its bounds. And that's what his elders and ancestors had repeated to him his entire life.

So, Pete was cautious about everything he did in this area. If he would make a new batch to sell, he had to sit, cook, watch, and shut down the entire operation. He could not go off and leave this running/cooking unattended. Therefore, he spent much time alone on this remote site, watching and listening for any sign to ensure his secret place was hidden.

Pete and Marcus had created a little parking area just off the main road on their property. When working up a batch of brew, they parked there and walked to the easement area. This was close enough that they could quickly carry supplies and hardware to and from the hidden site. If anyone asked, they said they put the parking area there so they could go hunting in their backwooded area and not have to carry anything for long distances from their house, located further west of this easement area.

Any car that came down the road, any horn honking, or any sound not made by nature was an alarm bell to Pete's ears. He was expecting Marcus to show up at some point and bring him something to eat while he spent the night getting this latest batch cooked up.

Pete heard that drip and sizzle sound again. '*Dammit,*' he thought, '*I'd better not be losing this precious product.*' As he squatted down and spread his legs, he looked under the main cooking tank and noticed a thin crack at the base and a little drop of his brew forming and dripping ever so slowly.

'*Well, great,*' he thought. He knew he'd been using this tank for about a year, so he knew it was probably getting close to ending its usefulness, but he didn't need that to happen right now. As he watched, the droplet formed at the base and slowly but surely fell into the open flame. He looked more closely and saw a tiny trickle of liquid soaking into the ground and forming a small pool, more like a little pothole or something. The collection had a strange green color, and whenever the liquid dripped onto the flame, it would sizzle but produce a tiny wisp of green fog. Pete thought that was strange because it smelled sweet and salty, like that smell he remembered from when he had gone to the adult bookstore in town and gotten his dick sucked by a hot female stripper. The whole place had that rancid yet exciting smell of sex.

Pete thought it strange that this green liquid/fog had that same smell. He kept watching the leak and decided it was minor enough not to cause an issue big enough to address with this "cook," but he would have to replace that tank and do it soon. And it was probably about time for him to relocate his "business" anyway, so this would incentivize him to find a new location while getting replacement parts to set up for operation again.

Although Pete saw the leak and the small amount of liquid dripping out of the tank, he figured it was minor. However, because of the darkness, he hadn't realized that the liquid he saw forming on the ground was only a portion of a larger pool beginning to collect behind the whole setup. This pool was down the hill from the still, and unless you looked closely at the scrub brush, you wouldn't notice the liquid that was trickling down to that pool or the pool itself, for that matter.

Pete shrugged, pulled out another cigarette, lit it, kicked the dirk where the liquid dripped, and covered up the little pool. That was a good enough solution for him at this time. He glanced at his watch and saw it was 8:30.

'Where the hell is Marcus? I'm getting hungry,' He thought.

At about that time, he saw what he thought were headlights and then heard a car door slam; he was on high alert. Although he was expecting his brother, one could never be too careful, so he hunkered down, waited, and watched. Worst case scenario, if need be, he could sneak off down the other side of the hill, run back into the woods, over a few yards, and come in the back way to where they kept their trucks parked behind another significant area of scrub brush. This was his escape hatch or capsule. He had never had to use this for emergencies but was happy it was an option, just in case.

As he squatted low and scanned the area toward the road, a big, burly man suddenly emerged from the darkness. It was Marcus, thank God. Pete chuckled as his racing heart slowly returned to its average speed. "Whew," he said as he wiped the sweat off his forehead, brow, and cheeks.

Marcus stood there in the glow of the cooking fire. At the age of 20, he was a mountain of a man. Marcus had shown an affinity for football and baseball while in high school. He wasn't worthy enough to land a full college scholarship but was good enough that some incentives existed.

Marcus stood at 6' 2" and was a walking muscle. He had a thick beard that he kept trimmed close to his chin. He didn't do the beard and mustache thing but only had the beard— sort of that Abe Lincoln chin-strap look. Marcus had a thickly muscled neck from years of football training and practice. He generally wore t-shirts and gym shorts or tight jeans. Marcus was not easy on clothing. His muscles flexed and protruded so much that it looked like his clothing was painted on his body. You could see every one of his eight-pack abs. He had hard nipples, like pencil erasers. Marcus's pecs pushed out and stretched the fabric of his shirt. He appeared to be a rough and gruff explorer out conquering the world but still had a boyish charm and a boyish fire in his eyes.

As Marcus came into the light of the fire, Pete found himself impressed with his little brother's stature. Pete might have been a little jealous but prided himself on knowing that his doing partly got Marcus to this state.

Marcus wore his typical t-shirt but must have come from the gym because he wore gym shorts. These were tight shorts, like the type of practice shorts a football player would wear when not playing the game. Those shorts didn't leave anything to the imagination. Pete noticed how Marcus's shorts clung to his massive hairy thighs. He could see the striations and bulges of Marcus's thick legs and ass as they seemed to fight the clothing he was wearing, close to, but not ripping with, every movement he made.

Pete often thought about the irony of ancestry and the physical characteristics people got from their family history. Although Pete was hairy from head to toe, Marcus wasn't quite as hairy. He was fuzzy, but the difference was that Marcus only had a slight dusting of hair on his chest. A few strands were growing around his pumped-up pecs and nipples, and a little bit between his pecs, but nothing else until you got just above his waist, and you'd see a thick protrusion of hair begin there and drift off into his pants.

Pete saw Marcus naked and knew that Marcus was covered in wavy or curly hair from his waist down his legs to his feet. Pete smirked and thought, *'Talk about a surprise. If you looked at Marcus, you'd think he was hairless until he takes off his shirt and or pants or wears shorts, and you see that there may not be a big forest up on top, but down low, look out, it's nothing but fur, no matter how far you look.'*

Marcus stood there with two twelve-packs of beer, a sandwich bag, and a pack of water bottles. The firelight bounced off his sweaty, glistening body as he slowly crept down the ridge toward the still. When he made eye contact with Pete, Marcus raised his hands as if presenting something for show and tell. Pete laughed and gave his brother a back-slapping hug, grabbed a beer as Marcus grabbed one, and they toasted and watched the fire continue to burn.

Pete and Marcus woofed down their sandwiches and cracked a 2nd beer each. Marcus suddenly heard that drip and sizzle sound as they sat there finishing their food and listening to the loud drone of crickets and bullfrogs. His attention was piqued. He glanced under the tank and saw the leak. He said, "Hey bro, you gotta leak."

Pete did an air-toast and said, "Yep, I saw that this evening. It's about time to replace this tank, but I think we've got a couple more uses out of it because the leak isn't huge yet."

Marcus nodded and said, "You're the big brother; you know about these things more than me." They both laughed and took a massive swig of their beer.

Again, because you had to watch the still when it was operational, Marcus planned to join Pete and spend the night getting this shine ready to distribute. They both had sleeping bags, and with the still fire to keep them warm and protected, they planned to lay down and spend the night. Of course, one brother would keep watch, and then they would rotate. This process had worked well, so it was a typical routine.

After cracking and finishing their 6th beer each, the brothers finally decided it was time to bed down. Again, Marcus would take the first watch since Pete had been there for some time already. Pete would bed down, and Marcus would sit, watch, and listen.

The brothers said their goodnights, and Pete was out like a light. It's good that neither of these boys snored because that would be a dead giveaway if someone snooped around.

Marcus sat listening to the drip and sizzle of that leaking tank. A couple of times, he caught himself dozing, jerking his head back off his chest, and yawning. That damned drip and sizzle were like the ticking of a clock, making it hard to stay awake.

Chapter Four

Little did they know that the hidden pool of leaking shine grew as Pete slept and Marcus fought to stay awake. Near the pool, if you listened closely, you could hear a subtle screeching noise, almost like someone cleaning the strings of an electric guitar with steel wool. It wasn't the typical high-pitched hum of a mosquito, but that sound came from what looked like mosquitoes. Their unearthly sound emanated as a chorus of squeaky off-key notes as they hovered, zigged, zagged, and zipped over and around this new pool. The water in the pool had a green tint, and it was thick, not like syrup, but it wasn't thin like regular water. Because the pool liquid was more viscous, it tended to form a very flat and glossy surface void of ripples or any other disturbances. This was a prime mosquito breeding environment.

Every so often, a bubble would form at the surface of this pool, and sooner or later, it would "burp," and a puff of green mist or gas would waft into the air. Because this was happening behind the still, neither brother saw it.

Anyone looking closely near this pool could see mosquitos breeding and laying their larvae in the pool. But, of course, the mosquitoes went about their business as usual. The uniqueness of the pool contents they were attracted to didn't mean much to them other than it was liquid and a safe place to breed.

The typical gestation period for a mosquito is 2 to 3 days from larvae to adulthood. These mosquitoes were laying their offspring on this Monday evening. Typically, by Wednesday, this group of hatchlings would be adults ready to annoy anything and everything they could. But were these normal mosquitoes?

Marcus's head dropped again, and his chin rested on his chest as his breathing began to slow. He was slowly falling asleep. Then, he suddenly popped his head up again, beat his chest with his fists, got up, walked over to the still, shook his legs, yawned again, and sat back down. He grabbed another beer and toasted the still, and guzzled it down.

Again, within a few minutes, his chin was courting with his pumped pecs. Finally, he was beginning to breathe rhythmically, and Pete woke up. He saw Marcus beginning to doze off and smacked Marcus's hairy thigh to snap him awake so he could let him know that he could now go to sleep and Pete would take watch. Marcus awoke with a start from the smack, and Pete just laughed.

Marcus scowled, crawled off his perch, and rested in his sleeping bag.

Pete was now wide awake.

Pete had perfected his cooking practice to the point where he knew how much wood to place under the tank, and it would burn and cook for the time specified. It would slowly burn down and out, and that timeframe seemed to work well for getting Pete the high-octane moonshine product that he and his friends and "customers" enjoyed from his brew. This made monitoring the still much more manageable. Once the fire was at peak performance, you didn't have to watch it constantly. The "magic" occurred during the cooldown, as the pressure tank would force compression, where all the alcohol came from. In effect, Pete had developed his scientific way of making a great brew. Who cares if it's illegal or not?

Besides Pete, everyone in both camps had finally bedded for the night. So, Pete was left staring at the fire embers and listening to the loud chorus of various night creatures chattering.

Chapter Five

Morning arrived. The sun slowly began to rise. There was still a mist or fog hovering over everything. Occasionally, a plume of green moisture would waft over the area. That same salty-sweet smell would also tend to come and go with those strange gusts.

I awoke with a start. I had been dreaming about something but wasn't sure what exactly. All I knew was that I had a raging piss hard-on and decided to get up, get out, and take care of that before the rest of the crew awakened. Because I was the senior member of our team, I volunteered to take the sleeping section of our tent where the main entrance was located. Unfortunately, this meant Brent, Roger, and Cliff would have to pass through my area to get out of the tent.

Logically, I felt it best to get out and take care of my morning condition before being caught and having to explain. Well, most of us already know what this means when it happens. Still, I didn't feel like joking about it or having it come up in conversation, especially considering my insecurity or embarrassment for having such a huge cock. Yeah, I know; that's my thing.

I tend to like to sleep nude, but I decided to sleep in my boxer briefs because the guys might need to pass by to get in or out of the tent. Let's just say that no matter how strong the fabric, a hard throbbing 11" cock is difficult to contain in a pair of shorts. I quickly pulled on my cargo shorts, socks, and boots, threw my shirt over my shoulders, and headed out of the tent to find a peaceful place to piss. My dick was still banging me left and right as I strode from camp to find an area secluded enough for me to kick back and let it all out.

As I left the tent, I could hear snoring. I wasn't sure where it came from, but I was glad everyone was asleep. When I got outside the tent, I looked at my watch and saw it was 6:00. The sun was starting to glow in the East, so there was enough light to see where I was going and what I was doing.

Roger and Brent climbed out of the tent when I returned to camp. Brent wore his cargo shorts, boots, and socks but still needed to throw on a shirt. He was at the camp stove and was starting to make coffee. I grunted a "morning" to him, walked to the office tent, and started looking at the charts and other materials to decide where to begin the day.

As I was reviewing documents and maps, Brent came in. He had thrown his shirt on but had left it untucked, and the three buttons at the top were open. His pecs, being thick as they were, caused his golf shirt to pull and stretch, which exposed most of the middle "cleavage" of his chest. The fur on his chest was already glistening with sweat. *'It's going to be another miserable, sweaty day,'* I thought. He handed me a cup of coffee and leaned near me to review the maps I was looking at. I could make out a slightly bitter-sweet smell and realized it had to be Brent's body odor. We were only on our second day in the field, and he was already starting to smell. Of course, I hadn't thought that I probably had a smell as well, but you know how we don't smell ourselves because we are used to it. So, I said nothing but hoped my team was not heavy, sweaty stinkers. I don't mind a manly scent, but I'm not into rancid smells, and I know some men can get rough smelling. The shower was installed but wouldn't be like some high-powered apparatus. Unfortunately, I feared we would all stink before this project was completed.

Roger had gone off to take care of "business." Brent and I reviewed and discussed the project scope and planned the day's work. As we were leaning over the maps we had, Brent said, "Have you seen that strange green fog or mist out there? It seems to come and go like wisps in the wind. I told him I had noticed it, but it seemed more prevalent than earlier. He and I both commented on the strange salty-sweet smell.

Just about that time, Roger pulled the tent flap back and strode into the office. He had his cup of brew as well. He was wearing his favorite threadbare jeans and his tight work shirt. He had on his ballcap and boots and was wearing his heavy-duty tool belt, ready to get busy. He greeted us, and we all raised our coffee mugs in salute.

Roger felt he should look after Cliff because Cliff was the young guy on the team. Roger made it a point to let us know Cliff was up and grabbing coffee and would be with us right away. Again, we all raised our mugs and saluted. Roger left the tent to assemble the equipment for our first trek into the wilderness.

The sun was beginning to show through the thick moss-covered trees, and we could already feel the heat and humidity rising. The constant chatter of crickets and frogs slowly tapered off as daylight began streaming through the trees and fog.

'This is going to be a thick and sultry day,' I thought as I shook my head and wiped my sweaty brow with a handkerchief.

I got up, and Brent and I left the tent and headed to get more coffee. Roger reported that he and Cliff had assembled our equipment, food, and water and were ready to head off into the muck to get this thing started.

We all downed our last sip of coffee and cleaned and tidied up the campsite, so when we got back all worn out, we wouldn't have to attend to the mess as well. I grabbed the charts and maps the office had given me to use in following our trek through the wilderness. Brent grabbed the instrument box, various writing materials, compass, and plumb bob.

Since Roger was the dedicated rod man, he carried the prism/poles, etc. Being the gopher, Cliff was saddled with taking anything else we couldn't get to. Each of us had a backpack with food and water provisions. So, we were well prepared for a few hours out in the field.

Since I wasn't carrying equipment, I was the guide who chopped the brush to get us through our survey process. Of course, we had to have a clear line of view whenever a shot was being made with the equipment, so someone would have to hack brush and tree limbs and anything else that might get in the way of the instrument being able to record coordinates via shooting to and from the prism.

Although we were in a very remote area, the scrub and brush were minimal. Our significant worries were more about the soggy floor conditions, the bugs, snakes, and crocodiles. But occasionally, I would have to chop a limb or hack a bush as we moved forward to set up our next shot. We had miles and miles of land to survey, so the sooner we could get a system down, the more efficient we would be because once we had a plan, it was a setup: shoot the shots, tear down, move forward, and repeat type of pattern.

We began by tying our shots to our encampment. You always need a beginning benchmark. We must find previously set markers to establish our site's beginning point.

This could mean we would trek for miles until we could see that first "known" point.

We took off along the known property line and began along an old fence. We must have been walking for about 30 minutes. I was hacking this and that shrub as the guys followed me into the wilderness. Finally, after what felt like miles and miles walked, we came upon a field marker set by a previous surveyor many years ago. This would be the benchmark for the beginning of our survey work.

Working from this point, located East of our home base, we could now work our way back to the West to find that marker. Once those markers were located and set, we would work north and record the rest of this vast parcel of land.

Recently, the land surveying process has embraced new technology whenever available. Newer surveyors can place markers at a property site with the surveyor's name, company name, certification license number, and other information. This would be recorded for future reference. I glanced at my charts and could locate this newer survey marker location based on my maps and charts. The match was perfect, so we knew where we were and the direction in which to proceed. Finding that one "needle in a haystack" could take some time on a survey, but once this was located, you could move quickly throughout the site, taking your shots and logging the data.

Finding that beginning marker point was generally the hardest thing to be done on a land survey project. Of course, this entire project would still be a sweaty, difficult task, but take away the stress and worry of finding that first marker point, and everyone can heave a heavy sigh of relief.

I have been on surveys where it took one or two days to find that first elusive marker point. So, I was exceedingly happy that we had already located that point. I thought, '*Way to go, team; you rock!*'

As we huddled near the point, recorded information, and began setting up the instrument, I noticed we were either damp or sweating so much that we would be wet come dinnertime. Brent had sweat soaking his shirt around his pits and even down near his belly, and his back was completely drenched. Thanks to all that fur that trapped moisture, I was sopping wet. Roger and Cliff both had some sweat, but I was surprised they weren't nearly as wet as us older guys. Oh, youth!

The guys had all learned this from me, but I noticed we wore tight handkerchiefs knotted into squares over our heads, followed by our ballcaps, etc. I remember the guys being thrilled when I showed them my little trick for helping to keep sweat from rolling in your eyes and stinging with all of its saltiness.

We continued moving along the site. Set up, shoot the shot, record the data, break down, move to the next point, and repeat. After a short period, the group would go into automatic mode. This same process would be repeated over and over again.

We moved west back toward our encampment along the property line. Finally, at around noon, we got to a small clearing in the thicket and decided this was an excellent time to settle down for lunch and try to cool off just a little bit. Although the sun shone through the clearing and was hot, the shade was along the peripheral. The benefit of the sun meant the ground was less soggy or soaked. Everyone dropped their backpacks, and we settled in a shady area with fallen trees. These made perfect benches. When you're out in the field, you make do with what you find.

We ate and shot the shit. Generally, when we would be on sites like this and would do everything together, we would always get into some small talk. Sometimes, it would be about this or that sports game, cars, hunting, etc. Sooner or later, the discussion would wind into a debate about women. We all had our say about the women in our lives or those who were no longer in our lives. I tend to shy away from these discussions, as this would sometimes bring bad energy to the group. I understand it can be destructive when breakups happen, and we are all here for our fellow man whenever that happens. However, I don't get into being around guys who sit and whine about the crap they've been through with their spouse or partner. I guess I tend to keep that emotional stuff to myself.

Lunch was good. Simple sandwich food and plenty of water. A slight breeze kicked up as we sat in the shade. It was refreshing. I could feel the sweaty areas on my shirt and shorts start to dry, but they still had the sweat stain patterns, and the fabric became crisper and stiffer. Sadly, this could end up becoming a skin-chafing nightmare. I made it a point to be aware of this because I hate getting heat rashes or skin irritations.

It looked like everyone else was drying out as well. *'Good,'* I thought, *'This will give everyone a little energy boost so we can continue to push through and work toward our goals.'*

After an hour of R & R, each guy moved off to his private spot, and we all relieved ourselves, packed up our stuff, and began moving to the next shot. The rest of the afternoon, we proceeded like this. Again, we made reasonably good progress, this being our first day.

Another issue when working on an extensive survey of this type was that you would move away from your encampment to take measurements and record data, but at the end of the day, you had to return to your campsite. This meant either retracing your steps or, if you were more aware of your location, you could try to cut corners and quickly cut back to the camp. Since we had so much to survey, we decided it would be best to retrace our steps back to camp for this first day. It just made more sense than trying to strike out in a new direction after being in the field all day and being hot and sweaty.

Since we had located the marker to the East and had begun working our way west to discover that second primary marker, we had crossed over the access road that led to our camp and proceeded to work our course west.

We stopped for the day and guessed our return trek would take us an hour or more, and that was walking, not doing any additional data finding. Finally, at about 6:00, we got back to camp. Everyone was exhausted, and we were all wet, clammy, and sweaty.

Of course, when camping, you can't just crack a beer, turn on the TV, and settle down in the A/C. So, there was still work to be done. First, we would need to clean up our equipment and prepare it for the next day. Next, we would need to pitch in to make dinner for all of us. Finally, we would get our sleeping areas neat and ready for a decent night's sleep.

By 8:00, we finally found the time to settle down next to our campfire. Since we were all tired, we laid off the night's booze and other party favors. As we sat around the fire, I mentioned how few bugs and mosquitoes we had encountered during our work today. Everyone chimed in and said they were glad we didn't have that extra nuisance. Everyone chuckled in agreement as we sat and gazed into the fire, almost as if we were hypnotized. That's what happens when you work hard in the field all day. When you sit down, your mind and body suddenly say, "TIME TO SHUT DOWN."

As we sat there, allowing the fire to burn its way out slowly, I caught Brent nodding his head a couple of times, and Roger did the same. Cliff was out there somewhere. I was surprised he wasn't being his same old prankster self. He was usually the most vocal of our group, always talking about some silly situation he or his friends got into. I couldn't put my finger on it, but something seemed amiss with Cliff on this trip. Not that I made it a point to worry about the personal lives of my team, but if someone acted way out of character, it would often make me stop and wonder if everything was okay. I decided to let it go for now, as my mind was tired of running all day, just like everyone else.

As the campfire ebbed to just coals smoldering, everyone started making motions to get ready to sleep. Since it was our first day out and we were exhausted, no one even considered taking a shower to get some of the sweaty grime off our bodies. The younger guys stated, "We are men, we smell like men, and we accept that." I'm not sure I was 100% on that same thought process, but I was also too tired to think about getting up, stripping, and washing with a trickle of water to rinse with.

The coals in the fire were stirred, and water was poured to ensure they were out. We left the citronella torches burning and all headed to the tent. After everyone had taken care of their personal needs, we each went to our respective sections of the sleeping tent. I turned on the A/C Unit to its lowest setting to help make sleeping better because we had to get our rest, or by the time this project was over, we would all need to recover in a mental ward. Rest was of the utmost importance.

I noted monitoring the battery source after this first night of running the portable A/C unit to see how badly it sucked the charge. As I made that mental note, I turned off my night light, plugged my devices in, set my alarm, and was off to Dreamland in no time. I had already become accustomed to the crickets and bullfrogs' drone outside and turned it into my white noise. Of course, I could generally sleep through anything, but crickets and frogs can get loud, so I just tricked my mind into thinking I had a white noise machine next to my bed and, "BOOM," I was out.

The rest of the night was uneventful.

Chapter Six

As Tuesday was winding down for the survey crew a few miles away, Pete and Marcus were lazily chilling out at their own "camp," so to speak.

From experience, when making a new batch of "brew," Pete knew you could not leave the still for very long because it needed to be monitored. It would be best to watch the smoke wafting from the fire and any steam or gasses that might be produced during the process. So, when Pete was "cooking," he was on site 100% of the time.

Being younger and less experienced in this process, Marcus became the "gopher" for the team. This meant Marcus was the one who ventured into town to grab food or anything else Pete might deem necessary to have while stationed at the site. In addition, Marcus would keep the house in decent shape, go to and from his job as a forklift driver for a local trucking and shipping company, and then at night; he would stop by to check up on his brother or sometimes spend the night. To Marcus, these "cooking" nights at camp would remind him of the fun they had had as kids when they went camping for no other reason but to camp out.

Pete and Marcus had finished cooling, bottling, and sealing the latest "brew" created. Pete was again beginning to get many orders for his product because of the reputation he and his dad had built. The Memorial Day Holiday would be coming up in a few weeks, and it seemed like Pete's regulars were placing larger orders and placing them more frequently.

Of course, this was Pete's business and a primary source of income, but being a good-ole-boy, he didn't keep the most outstanding accounting books. Pete completely overlooked the difference in the output of this batch to notice several pints were missing. Of course, this was due to the leaky tank, but Pete missed the clue.

Pete decided to turn around and start another fresh batch to cook Tuesday and into Tuesday night. He didn't always cook one batch right after another, but he couldn't pass up this opportunity with orders coming in and Marcus and he both being able to use the money they would make. So, this would mean another night spent on site, watching for anybody snooping around and maintaining the fire so his prized product would come out as delicious as previous batches. After all, Pete did have a reputation to uphold.

Marcus helped Pete get the last batch processed. He and Pete loaded the back of his truck with the latest brew. They covered it with a tarp so as not to draw attention, and Marcus made sure to drive all speed limits and follow all laws. Getting stopped with this sort of contraband would seriously ruin Marcus's life. Pete tried everything he could to keep

Marcus out of the loop as much as possible. Pete wanted Marcus to break this cycle, go to college, get a degree, and make something out of himself. So, Pete tried to get by without much help from Marcus. However, running a moonshine still just isn't easy for one person, so unfortunately, Pete still needed Marcus's help now and then.

Once Marcus returned to the house and unloaded the new brew into their storage shed, covered in tarps and under lock and key, he ran to the convenience store and grabbed a couple of sodas, another two twelve-packs of beer, and some deli sandwiches. He was planning to spend the night on-site with Pete again tonight.

Marcus had already been approved for the rest of the week off for vacation time to enjoy some R&R and chill out. This was a slow time for shipping products, so instead of rolling around the shipping warehouse either sweeping or finding something else to keep busy, he decided to use up some of his OT comp time. He should be well-rested and ready for shipments to ramp up again in June. Taking time off also allowed Marcus to help his older brother out as much as possible. Marcus didn't see his involvement with the moonshine business as bad. Still, being younger, he hadn't considered the consequences if he were to be arrested and booked for possession of illegal contraband. So, Marcus did everything within his power to be there for his brother. After all, his brother had been there for him for all those years after their folks were killed; helping Pete was the least Marcus could do.

The sun was beginning to hang lower in the sky when Marcus finally made his way back to camp at around 7:30. When Marcus walked up to camp, he saw Pete sitting in a chair with his head down, apparently taking a nap, even though he said he was ALWAYS alert when cooking.

Marcus chuckled to himself. He thought about walking up behind Pete and scaring him, but as much fun as that would be, Marcus knew he'd pay for that trick for some time to come, and on this hot, muggy day, he didn't have the energy to set himself up by jumping and scaring his brother. He decided the best approach would be to snap some twigs and branches, which would stir Pete. After the second twig was snapped, Pete was wide awake and looking around. He saw Marcus and jumped with a start at first but then calmed down.

It's a good thing Marcus didn't play the scare prank on his older brother. Unbeknownst to Marcus, his older brother had installed a few "boobytraps" at various locations on the property. He had learned some of these trap types from listening to his dad tell stories about war times. When younger, he had made this his research project and checked out books at the library to learn how to make a trap work. He had set some traps mainly to see if he could get them to work the way everyone said they would, but he also felt this was another way to create a sense of safety or security around this location. He never told Marcus about this because he didn't want that to become standard information. He would caution Marcus not to go walking off into the property because of the swamp, critters, and bugs. Marcus wasn't an outdoorsman like Pete, so he didn't have to be told twice.

But Pete did suffer from some form of PTSD, so it's not that Marcus would step into a trap, but Pete had also set traps because he felt he always needed to be aware of his surroundings or at least have his backside protected. Again, this came from listening to his dad's old war stories.

Marcus was aware of Pete's "jumpiness," so he laughed and said, "Yeah, I'm ALWAYS alert when cooking." Pete glared at him, wiped his sleep-puffed face, grabbed the case of beer, spit on the ground, and gave a gruff huff to show his annoyance at Marcus's little joke.

The second cook was in process. Pete had already inspected the pressure tank and had determined it wouldn't last much longer, so that's another reason why he decided to cook another batch so soon. With the money he would bring in for the recently produced batch, he would have enough spare cash to drop for a new cook tank. But, depending on supplies, it could take a few weeks to acquire, set up, and start using the new tank, so this last batch was critical to keep the supply chain moving. If people can't get the illegal contraband they want and are willing to pay for, they will move on to the next available supplier. So, it was vital if you were a reputable "shiner" that you kept the interest of your clientele in check and you readily had the product for them whenever the need arose.

As Marcus joined Pete near the still. They sat, each cracked open a beer, and ingested the sandwiches Marcus had brought.

Pete had positioned himself to watch the pressure tank more closely. He could still see the drip and hear the sizzle as some of the "brew" would hit the open flame. The dripping from the cook tank was growing, but Pete felt it wasn't enough of a leak to cause him not to try to create this last batch. A little loss was typical with any process. This came from the guy who missed the considerable product loss from his most recent collection of Shine.

Even though they were now aware of and monitoring the leak from the cook tank, Pete and Marcus were only mindful of the pool formed from the last batch cooked a couple of days earlier. And even though the leak was continually adding more liquid to the developing fluid collection, the pool's surface was still smooth like glass. To the mosquitoes who were now happily laying eggs and watching the new hatchlings grow into adulthood, this was a Shangri-la. No pests were attacking them, and they went into hyper mode, continually laying more and more eggs.

The first generation of mosquitoes spawned from this pool looked different than a typical mosquito. If scientists had been present, they would have wanted to capture and study this strange breed of the common blood-sucking pest. They had the same body shape as a typical mosquito, but the new breed of hatchling seemed much more significant than your typical mosquito. Fully grown, these weird mosquitoes appeared to be about one and a half times the size of the regular pest, but an even more unique identifier was that these larger specimens had a shiny greenish hue to their bodies. Sort of that vibrant green color of a June Bug. Could this result from them forming in this green pool of thick liquid? Scientists would be putting their little heads together to try to answer this question and more if they knew what was happening in the wetlands.

As this new generation of pests developed their "hunting" legs, so to speak, they began swarming the pool. The sun was still out, and although mosquitoes don't generally seem to have a specific feeding time, they tended to wait until sundown or after to kick their blood-sucking appetites in gear.

Maybe it was hereditary for them to wait until dawn, dusk, or dark to feed so that they could come and go and hover around their victims virtually unseen in the darkness. Additionally, these strange new mosquitoes still had that quiet singing effect when flitting and drifting. The sound was that strange guitar string screeching, but at an even higher pitch, where sometimes you thought you heard something but weren't entirely sure it was real because the sound came and went so infrequently. This made it even harder for victims to listen to these attackers when approaching to chow down on prime red-blooded hosts.

Pete and Marcus were on their 8th beer each. Their bellies were full, and they each lit a cigarette and stared into the open flames. Finally, Pete pulled out a joint and lit it. If they were stuck out here in the wilderness with minimal entertainment, they might as well drink, smoke, and enjoy the moment.

Pete lit the joint, sucked in the smoke, and passed it to his younger brother as he exhaled. "Man, I love that first toke," he thought. Marcus leaned over, grabbed the joint, and took a deep draw. He handed it back to Pete and exhaled. They smiled at one another and continued this pattern while watching the fire.

Marcus suddenly perked up and told his brother he had recently met this incredible chick. He said she was kinky, and they had had some awesome sex already. Pete chuckled at Marcus's giddy mood. Pete thought, '*Ah, young love.*'

As they sipped beer and smoked, Marcus commented again about how kinky this chick was. He said she had introduced him to some illegal substances that he found intriguing. During sex one night, she had presented him with a little brown bottle of liquid. He just looked at it, and she explained it was something called "poppers" on the streets. She explained it wasn't a severe drug, but if you took a whiff or two through your nose, it would make you feel like you were blasting off into the stars. As she slowly sat down on Marcus's throbbing cock, she took a couple of whiffs and held the bottle under his nose, and had him breathe. Marcus laughed again and said, "Man, that's the best orgasm I think I've ever had." Pete grinned and was intrigued by this. Pete wasn't much on drugs. He was okay with booze and pot, but those were natural things, for the most part, and if God deemed them to be created naturally, then man should be able to use them "naturally" as well.

Marcus continued his discussion and said this girl he was seeing had also given him some "special" pills. She said if you laced anyone's drink with one of these pills, they would become so out of it that they would do anything you told them to do. Marcus thought this was kinky and crazy. Being a naïve Southern boy, he had no idea there were substances out there that could cause someone to obey another without fighting back. He professed he had the pills with him but wasn't sure what to do with them and would hold onto them since they could come in handy.

Pete asked why this girl was so generous with her "drugs." Marcus said she had told him she had gotten many of these from a friend and honestly didn't know what to do with them, so she thought she'd share.

Pete felt it strange that she would freely give these pills away, but he could only think, '*I'm not going to drink anything you give me again.*' He vowed then and there that he would not accept anything edible from Marcus. Not that there was any worry Marcus would do something sneaky like that, but the thought of him becoming subservient to his younger brother was not appetizing.

Marcus ended his discussion by laughing again and then saying he wasn't sure he'd keep seeing this girl because she was kinkier than anyone he had ever known, and he thought of himself as being pretty damned kinky. He also said she was really into open relationships and group activities with others, and he wasn't sure he wanted to go that route. He also wasn't sure he wanted to worry every time he had sex with her that she might go overboard on her kinky side, or worse, she has caught something that she would share during sex that he would not want to have after the sex act had occurred—namely, an STI.

Pete sat gazing at the fire, shaking his head. Marcus joined him, shaking his head and chuckling.

The food, beer, and joint relaxed both brothers. It was a quiet night. Sure, the crickets and bullfrogs were back at it again, but otherwise, it seemed to be a calm night. In no time, both brothers sitting in their camp chairs reclined a little, with their heads tipped down and their chins slowly meeting up with their chests as they started to doze.

As Pete and Marcus dozed, feeling warm and fuzzy, the strange sound of a high-pitched screeching guitar could suddenly be heard above the brothers, then another, and another, all hovering in the air.

As the insects were zipping back and forth and hovering, their sound would come and go, almost like a radio station gaining and losing its signal. A person would have to sit still and listen actively to hear one of these mosquitoes getting ready to attack its prey.

The time for the swarm of this new breed of mosquito to attack was upon the brothers.

Pete and Marcus sat, legs spread wide, heads down, sweating and breathing deeply. Every so often, the slightest breeze would waft over the camp, causing the brothers to subconsciously spread their knees or wave their legs back and forth to try and capture as much cool air as possible and funnel it up to their sweaty loins. The warm, humid night and the beer relaxed the brothers and lulled them into a deep sleep.

Marcus wore his typical gym shorts, tight t-shirt, hiking boots, and socks. And he was never seen without his ball cap. He'd turned his ballcap backward like the "cool" dudes do. The brim of his hat gently heaved up and down, casting a shadow across the back of his neck. As he dozed in his chair, one of the giant green mosquitoes appeared and began to hover over him. Marcus rested deeply, and his slumbering ears didn't detect the steely screeching guitar sound. Next, there were two more of them approaching. The off-key harmony of multiple "skeeters" hovering would have been the perfect soundtrack for some creepy slasher movie thriller, at least during those sporadic moments when you could hear something. The first mosquito slowly dropped, nearing the warm, sweaty smells of this man sleeping before it. The mosquito dropped lower near Marcus's thigh. As Marcus sat resting, his legs spread wide; he had absentmindedly pulled the legs of his shorts higher on his thighs, again to try and gain a little reprieve from this intense humidity. Marcus's shorts were hiked up his legs, and it was now easy to view up the leg of his shorts into the shadows where you could see his jockstrap, furry thighs, and the bulge his cock was making.

The mosquito hovered, riding the waves of heat emanating from Marcus's crotch as he rocked his knees back and forth to fan his crotch more. Ensuring its prey would not attack, the giant mosquito swooped near Marcus's shorts and flew up the leg opening. The air inside Marcus's shorts was hot, salty, and sweaty. Marcus usually wears floppy shorts to ensure his "manhood" is as ventilated as possible. This allowed for a nice open space inside the crotch of his shorts, which allowed his genitals to "breathe." The mosquito hovered just over the crotch of Marcus's jockstrap. Suddenly as the mosquito landed on Marcus's jock, it began prodding with its larger-than-normal proboscis, slowly sticking it into the fabric of the jock. Marcus moved a little, and the mosquito took a flight to be ready to vacate the area if necessary. Marcus settled back down, and the mosquito landed again. This time it moved quickly over the jockstrap and stopped right where Marcus's dickhead was under the fabric. The mosquito pulled out the long spike it uses to feast on its prey and jabbed it deeply into the material, piercing the skin on the head of Marcus's dick with a stinging pinch.

Suddenly, Marcus woke up, jumped, grabbed his crotch, and moaned deeply. '*What the fuck was that,*' he thought. It felt like his dick had suddenly been dipped in molten lava and was on fire. He got up, shook each of his legs, grabbed his crotch again, and shook it. The burning seemed to subside just a little bit. Finally, Marcus decided maybe it was just that feeling you get when you need to piss. So, he walked away from camp into the scrub, pulled out his dick, and pissed a long hot stream onto the ground. *'Damned beer,'* he thought.

As he held his dick and pissed, Marcus felt a bump forming at the head of his dick, and it was starting to swell and itch. *'Goddammit,'* Marcus thought. *'Damned mosquito bite right on the tip of my dick. You asshole, you had to bite me there,'* he thought as he casually began to rub the head of his dick while finishing off the urine stream. All he kept thinking was how this had better not put him out of commission on the sex scene because he was planning to get busy this coming weekend. After all, why not? He'd be collecting a nice little payment from this current batch of brew he and his bro would sell.

Marcus huffed under his breath, "Damned freaking skeeters." And then he spat on the ground.

Through all of this, Pete continued to lay still and sleep. He must have been more relaxed because he knew Marcus was here and they would look out for each other. Another one of the strange mosquitoes hovered over his chest, zipping and darting, always alert and ready to be swatted away instantly. As Pete's chest heaved up and down from his deep breathing, the mosquito landed on his chest. Pete was wearing his typical T-shirt and jeans. The mosquito started prodding with that larger-than-normal proboscis. Suddenly, it moved over on top of Pete's left nipple. Pete's nipples were hard under his shirt. He must have been having a hot dream or something. As his chest moved rhythmically with his breathing, the mosquito stung him right through the fabric of his shirt and into his nipple.

Just as Marcus had done earlier, Pete jumped and swatted his chest. But unfortunately, his left nipple also felt like it had been dipped in molten lava. His nipple was on fire and stinging, and it started to itch. Pete thought, '*DAMNED MOSQUITOES,*' as he began to rub his nipple. This caused the pain to subside a little.

Pete didn't see Marcus and figured he had gone off to take a piss. Sure enough, Marcus came out of the darkness just as he thought this. He was walking funny and kept grabbing and rubbing his crotch. Pete thought Marcus looked funny walking with his legs spread open and constantly grabbing his crotch and stroking it.

Pete got up, nodded at his brother, and walked in another direction to find a nice, quiet place to wet the ground with his urine. He mindlessly went through the darkness until he felt he was far enough away from camp. He opened his jeans and let loose with a long hard stream of piss. Standing there holding his dick and pissing, he absentmindedly began rubbing, scratching, and caressing his left nipple. After pissing, he returned to the still and the fire. Finally, he got to where he could see by the firelight and pulled up his shirt.

Sure enough, a well-formed bite was swelling and reddening on the areola at his nipple.

Marcus was still moving around in an agitated state, rubbing his crotch and moaning. Pete noticed, after he had been rubbing the pain out of his nipple that he would moan every so often. *'That's not like me; my nipples have never been sensitive; what the heck,'* he thought. He absentmindedly kept gently caressing the left side of his chest and giggled as he watched Marcus jumping around and scratching or rubbing his crotch like a crazed animal.

Marcus noticed Pete laughing, stopped, and said, "Man, oh man, what sort of fucking skeeter bite is this?

Pete looked Marcus in the eye and pointed to his left nipple and scratched and pointed to Marcus's crotch, and just as he did that, Marcus scratched and thumbed the crotch of his shorts again. Not that Pete cared to notice, but it did seem like Marcus's dick was growing in his shorts. He looked at Marcus again and said, "Quit rubbing it, or you're going to shoot in your shorts." They both laughed and settled back down, each grabbing another beer.

Every so often, one or other of the brothers would absentmindedly scratch or rub their respective bites, and slowly but surely, their beers were emptied, and, once again, both of their chins began to make dates for a rendezvous with their chests. Sure enough, they were both out and breathing contentedly.

More sounds of scalding liquid burning on the open flame as it dripped from the failing cook tank. These strange mosquitoes began laying eggs in the green pool, only to be met with more larvae growing to maturity, hatching, and flying up to hover with the ever-growing mass of this new breed of pest. The pests seemed more focused on procreating and drifting than doing much more biting now. Pete and Marcus were lucky to be sitting a little bit downwind of the still; thus, the smoke from the cook fire was gently wafting around them. Sometimes, it would still have that green appearance, but none of this bothered the brothers as they fell into a deep sleep.

Everyone in both encampments finally bedded down and was lulled to sleep by the crickets and frogs, but the busy movements and growing number of "KWEER Skeeters" were increasing rapidly.

Chapter Seven

Morning came sooner than anyone wanted, of course.

The morning sky lightened, and I began to stir in the sleeping tent. Again, I could hear snoring in a couple of the other areas of the tent. I didn't know who it was and didn't care. The snoring seemed to add another chord to the already loud chatter of the swamp's early morning orchestra of sounds.

I got up and threw on my shorts and work shirt from yesterday. They didn't smell great, but it wasn't so bad that I couldn't wear them again for another day. Since I was up early, I made it my task to make coffee for the team. I got it going, grabbed my first cup, and headed to the office tent.

I sat down, turned on the database equipment, and reviewed the previous day's entries. Reviewing the information, I noted some discrepancies I wasn't happy to see. Again, when surveying, any deviations from the recorded markers can become skewed, and as you move forward with the survey, this variation can cause the data to become compromised. I scratched my head and kept reviewing the documentation. It wasn't terribly off, but I still wasn't happy with what I saw.

Brent pulled back the flap of the office tent and sauntered in, coffee cup in one hand and rubbing his eyes with the other. He grinned, saluted with his coffee cup, and sat across from me at the desk. He said, "Mornin. You have a scowl; anything I need to know about?"

I wasn't aware that I had been making a face, but I guess it was just the face of frustration because I didn't like the thought that we might have to retrace our steps if the data was inaccurate. I nodded to Brent and explained what I was seeing. His facial expression changed as well. He took on a slight brooding look and rubbed his forehead. I told him it wasn't a huge issue, but we needed to resolve it now, or the rest of our survey would be corrupted, which would end up wasting more and more time if it wasn't corrected early on.

I could think of no quicker or better solution than to stop and review what we had already recorded. I sat back in my folding chair and said to Brent, "So here's what we need to do to fix this." Brent leaned forward, sipped his coffee, and attentively listened.

It appeared Brent had also decided wearing yesterday's clothing was okay because as he leaned over to review the data, I got a strong whiff of musky, sweaty man scent. You know, sort of like going to a gym that has rarely been cleaned. The musky smell of sweat and other body odors permeates the walls if not kept clean.

I didn't react visibly to Brent's smell, but it was intense. I'm sure I didn't smell great either, so maybe our scents would cancel one another out.

As we reviewed the documentation, I told him he and I would need to stay at camp this morning and figure out what had caused this "break" in our data collection. This would require us to review the digital data, examine the survey instruments to ensure they were calibrated correctly, and see if we could find where the error had occurred. From experience, I knew this was the best option, and from experience, I was confident we would see the mistake and not have to retrace our steps. This required a little time to focus and follow our recorded path, and the error would present itself.

Since time is money and we were all on the clock during business hours, I felt uncomfortable with Roger and Cliff sitting around while Brent and I tried to solve this issue. Having four guys reviewing documentation is like that old saying, "Too many cooks in the kitchen." So, I told Brent that once Roger and Cliff were up and active, we would send them west along the property line to ensure we had a clear path to work on for our next day of data collection. I figured if Brent and I needed to take half a day to review and fix this problem, I would have the young guys head off and chop and clear the property lines so we wouldn't lose as much time and would be able to pick up and progress with the survey and not have to spend time chopping and clearing as we surveyed and could push through the setup and tear down routines and move along more quickly. So, we might be losing time this morning by not picking up and moving forward, but we weren't losing time because the guys could be doing background work to keep us on schedule.

This would also be a great training process for Roger and Cliff. I was effectively instilling my trust in them to perform the assigned tasks, and they would be doing it without my or Brent's immediate supervision. I felt this would be a good test to help educate both younger men on taking responsibility for their actions and doing the job before them, not "squirreling" around and wasting valuable time.

Roger and Cliff strolled into the tent with their mugs steaming as they sipped and nodded at Brent and me. They both had a disheveled look, probably because they hadn't performed a regular morning routine with showering, shaving, etc. Once I knew I had everyone's attention, I explained the issues I had discovered and how we would attack this before it became an issue none of us could correct.

I sipped the remainder of my coffee and said, "Roger, you and Cliff are going to take the machetes and radios, and I want you to head west along the property line and clear everything out so once Brent and I figure out this issue, we can pick up and get right back to it." I told Roger and Cliff they really wouldn't need much equipment. Unfortunately, most of their work today would involve chopping and clearing. They wouldn't need a bunch of equipment to perform manual labor.

I reminded them to ensure they took plenty of water with them. Food wasn't as important, although necessary when wandering in dense wooded, swampy areas; you most certainly need to stay hydrated.

Roger and Cliff looked at one another, then back at me, shook their heads in affirmation, and said they were here to do a job; this was just another aspect of their job description. I was pleased that they seemed to take this task in stride.

Based on the review of our existing maps, I advised that the boys should make it to our property's corner by mid-afternoon. I recommended that once they reach the corner of our property, they spend a little extra time to see if they can locate the property marker. I advised them not to disturb anything where the marker is supposed to be discovered but to keep an eye out because this will make our jobs much easier if they find it, and we can pick up and continue our survey during the upcoming days.

I also advised them to pay attention to crossing fences or other manufactured items to ensure they kept on the correct path, stayed on our property, and did not encroach on a neighboring property. I wasn't overly concerned because the boys wouldn't be processing survey data. However, I still didn't want them wasting time accidentally crossing over to another piece of property that had no connection with our survey. Again, this would be a mistake that could cause this survey to take even longer. And, as stated before, "Time is Money."

We grabbed a hearty breakfast and finished our coffee, and Brent and I helped load up Roger and Cliff and sent them off on their way. I advised them to radio Brent or me immediately if they saw anything or anything happened. They nodded again, double-checked their equipment, tested their radios, and headed opposite the rising sun.

We watched the boys walking west and growing smaller as they moved farther away from us; Brent made another pot of coffee. We glanced at one another over fresh steaming cups of java and headed back to the office tent to figure out where we had a "bust" in our data. Both of us secretly hoped this task would not be an all-day one.

As we re-entered the tent, I noticed the tent had already started to take on that gym locker room smell. You know that pungent, if not rancid, smell of men sweating. I was, again, shocked at just how fast we had all begun to produce those manly smells and how those smells were already permeating the inside of the tent. I tried to put the thought out of my mind at just how bad this smell was going to be if we were, in fact, out in the field on this project for several weeks.

'Well,' I thought, *'It's part of the job, and we all just have to be men and suck it up.'*

It was about 9:00, and Brent and I had been reviewing data for about an hour. We had yet to turn on the A/C unit because I was concerned about how much power they would use and didn't want us to sacrifice anything else to keep it a bit cooler in the tent. As I leaned near Brent and glanced at one list of data, sweat dripped off my brow and splashed onto Brent's hairy forearm. We made eye contact briefly, and I said, "UM, sorry, man." He laughed, wiped off the sweat, slapped me on the back, and said, "All part of the job, man." We laughed at that, and I got up and turned on the A/C unit.

As the tent began to cool slightly, we sat next to one another so there were two sets of eyes on the data. I was thankful for the A/C, but it just took the edge off the heat and humidity. Both Brent and I were already beginning to show sweat on our shirts and shorts. As we sat next to one another, our knees touched under the desk. Neither of us let on as if we had even noticed. I felt Brent move his knee away from mine as he leaned closer to me to review one data string.

At noon, Brent suddenly dropped his hand to the sheets we reviewed and said, "AH HA, I think I've found the issue." As we continued to review the data, Brent pointed out what he had seen. The error was evident at that point. We quickly made corrections to our data, but just to be safe, I wanted to recalibrate all of our instruments to ensure there would be no further discrepancies in the data we collected and whether this was human error or not, I decided at this time of the day it would be best just to set up and test everything so we don't have any future setbacks.

With lunch and instrument work, the rest of the day would be spent getting everything back in order. However, I was still confident the boys would return at the end of the day, and tomorrow, we would have a nice clear patch to follow based on their hard work. That should keep us from losing any productive time, as we should be able to shoot the data much quicker since the boys will have already cleared our path.

Brent and I broke up for lunch. Sitting near the dormant fire pit, he and I saw more of that strange green fog wafting through the moss-covered trees. Brent pointed it out to me, and I said, "I have seen that several times. Do you think it is some form of swamp gas or something?" Brent gulped his soda, shook his head, and said, "I've never seen anything like it. It doesn't appear harmful, but it is strange." That was the last we discussed the fog.

After lunch, we returned to the office tent to recalibrate the instruments and verify our data. It was nearing 4:00 in the afternoon, and Brent and I surmised the boys would return to camp shortly. Once we had finished with all the equipment and all had been placed back where it belonged, Brent and I decided we'd start getting camp ready for dinner.

We grabbed more branches and various kindling and set up our evening's fire pit. We decided we wouldn't start dinner until the boys returned, but at least we had everything ready. I was so thankful for Brent always being on his best game and discovering where our data errors had occurred. I try not to let this job stress me out, but sometimes, I do fret if I can't figure out what is causing an issue. However, I felt relaxed knowing that my stress had been reduced by half because of Brent's alert diligence.

We sat, sipped water, and waited for the boys to return to camp.

Now that we had settled down from our busy work routine, I suddenly noticed the sky growing dark. I thought, '*I didn't check the weather patterns this morning.*' There had been no warnings or forecasts for severe weather; however, this being Florida, it is not unusual for a quick, nasty thunderstorm or windstorm to blow up out of nowhere on a hot, humid afternoon.

The wind began to pick up, and off in the distance to the west of us, I thought I heard thunder. Suddenly, I was apprehensive about the boys. We sent them out into the field today and hadn't checked the weather because no one expected anything severe. They hadn't even taken their rain ponchos or anything. I mentioned this to Brent, and he quickly came to my defense and said things were a bit chaotic this morning due to the data breach, so the weather was not on anyone's mind. Brent said he had confidence that the boys could take care of themselves if they got hit by a storm but also reassured me that they had their radios, so if something did happen, they could contact us to let us know.

As the winds continued increasing and the sky darkened, I was sure I had heard thunder. Quickly, out of nowhere, there was a flash of lightning and an almost instant crash of thunder that shook the ground in our campsite. A massive gust of wind swooped over our camp. Luckily, everything seemed to stay intact, but when Brent and I started to feel the rain, we hopped up and ran for the office tent to double-check and ensure the equipment was safe and dry.

I hoped the boys were okay or could seek shelter from this crazy storm.

Chapter Eight

Morning arrived, and it was so calm and comfortable sleeping that I just wanted to roll over and return to sleep. Unfortunately, Cliff's alarm went off just as I started to doze. '*I'm up,*' I thought to myself. I bolted out of bed and dressed in the same clothes I wore yesterday; yeah, so what? They are sweaty, but as long as I'm not offended by my smell, neither should anyone else be offended. Once we had splashed water behind our ears, we ran to the "most powerful" coffee throne and grabbed our morning brew.

As Cliff and I entered the office tent, we noted that Tom and Brent seemed to be frowning. I've known these two guys for a few years, so I've become pretty attuned to their expressions and instantly knew something was amiss. I glanced at Tom and Brent, raised my coffee mug, sipped, and nodded my good morning. They looked up and responded, but both continued to frown.

Cliff didn't seem to be aware of what was happening until Tom informed us that Cliff and I would spend the day chopping and clearing a path to the West of our camp because there was an issue with the previous day's data collection. We could not collect more data until the error was located and corrected. Brent informed us that they would also recalibrate all the instruments to ensure no more issues as we continued this project.

Tom looked me in the eye and proceeded to give me instructions. He advised that I would be in charge of our small sub-team. He advised us to get our equipment and gear in order and told us to start moving west and try to return to camp by 6:00. I liked feeling like Tom trusted me enough to give me more authority than I had ever had. This was a test to see if Cliff and I could complete any task we were instructed to do quickly and efficiently.

I was excited to be given the responsibility and that Cliff and I could get out and do our job and do it well but also not feel like our superiors were constantly watching us. And above all, they trusted us to perform our duties with minimal supervision. That made me want to put a feather in my cap and pat myself on the back. It's always inspiring when your leader or supervisor indicates they respect you enough to give you authority.

It looked like the day would be another hot, sticky, sweaty one with lots of sun and haze, so Cliff and I packed the machetes and other brush-cutting and chopping tools. We loaded up on water and took backpacks along that contained our lunches. Tom and Brent checked the status of our radios to ensure that if anything did happen, we would all be able to contact one another.

No one was thinking about rain protection or anything like that. After all, it's always hot and damp when in the swamp, so a quick rain shower is generally appreciated because it's like taking a cold shower on Mars, where you'd have that one spot of refreshment while inside a broiling oven and carrying one less piece of equipment or clothing while walking for miles is always welcome.

After all of the systems had been checked, and equipment had been verified, Cliff and I took off, with me leading the way. I waved back at Tom and Brent and said, "See ya at dinner time." They laughed as they turned and headed back into the office tent to try and figure out where the error had occurred.

Cliff and I took off in a Westward direction. We only had one compass between us, but that was okay because there was no thought of us being separated, as our mission for the day was to take off in the correct direction and cut and move the brush. So, it wasn't like we needed complete accuracy. As we cleared, we needed to stay on the right side of the property, so I was constantly watching for any crossing fences or strange land markings that might signify a different parcel of land that didn't belong to our lot.

Cliff seemed quiet again today. I wasn't going to push him for information, but it was strange that he wasn't cutting up and trying everything he could to prank one or more of us on this trip. As we continued our Westward trek, we didn't say much other than to point out this or that bush, tree limb, or sapling that needed to come down to ensure we would have a clear path for the following day. A couple of times, Cliff seemed angry with the shrub or limb he was attacking and would almost seem to go "madman" on them. He would grunt and breathe heavily, and the poor limb or shrub would be massacred.

After a couple of hours of this behavior, as we stopped for a water break, I casually asked if everything was okay with Cliff. He took a swig of his water, looked in my direction, grunted, and then said, "G'damned bitch I've been dating for the past few months dumped me this past weekend after I told her I would be away from my phone for a few days and possibly weeks due to work. She didn't believe me, accused me of cheating, and nothing I could say or do would prove to her that I wouldn't be out partying but would be working."

"Good riddance," Cliff yelled. "Who needs a fucked-up pussy when we have more manly goals to strive for." Internally, I disagreed with Cliff's ideology, but I just shook my head, said I was sorry, and said, "Yep, that's the way the cookie crumbles." We saluted our waters and returned to the chore at hand. I will be honest and say I was a little happy that Cliff was down. Maybe this would mean none of us would bear the brunt of his prank jokes or fart attacks. Fingers crossed.

We continued to hack at the brush and keep our bearings to avoid straying from the current property line. By lunchtime, we had only made it about one and a half miles. Even though yesterday's survey work seemed relatively straightforward, there was more undergrowth west of our home base than I think either Tom or Brent knew. By the time lunch rolled around, Cliff and I had sore arms and shoulders and were drenched in sweat, literally from head to toe. Again, we used Tom's technique of placing tied-up handkerchiefs under our ballcaps to help catch all the sweat our heads produced. This technique worked well, at least for keeping sweat out of one's eyes. This did not help with the rest of our wet and sweaty bodies.

Cliff and I broke up for lunch. We sat and shot the shit as we chewed on sandwiches and sipped our water. Cliff brought up his ex-girlfriend again. He apologized for not being himself but said this hurt because he thought she might be "the one." Now, he was seeing red flags. I told him this is all part of the game, and how you play that game proves if you are a winner or a loser, but everyone wins at something or other in life. On that last notion, I could see Cliff's eyes light up, and his demeanor seemed to change. He seemed to lighten his expression and became more animated as he said, "You know what, 'OLD MAN,' you are right on this subject."

I felt my face flush as I realized I was advising a young man who wasn't much younger than me but who seemed to look up to me as a knowledgeable and experienced man. I was shocked because I also realized, '*Hey, wait a minute, now I'm starting to feel like that elder that young people respect and worship.*'

With that notion, it was back to work. So, I hopped up, stowed my lunch remnants, and we took off again. I had noticed or thought I had seen, that the sky was darkening the further west we moved. I didn't recall anyone in camp saying anything about stormy weather or anything like that. Of course, having lived in Florida for a long time, I was never surprised by a pop-up rainstorm or thundershower. Considering the data issue at camp this morning, I wasn't surprised that none of us consulted the tent's weather reports that came in via the office communication connection. I figured it was probably because this data discrepancy flustered Tom. Heck, none of us wanted to redo this work again, so it was understandable that we tried to figure out the error, correct it, and ensure this wouldn't continue as we moved forward with our work. And when working on critical data issues, sometimes things like the weather fall to the back burner.

By 3:00, Cliff and I had made it another mile along our property line. The wind was beginning to pick up, and the Western sky was turning black. Neither Cliff nor I had packed any rain gear because we weren't expecting rain or storms. The saving grace is that it is hot out, so getting rained on wouldn't make us cold, but having hot, wet, sweaty clothes made wetter by rain in humid conditions certainly did not help anything.

I stopped Cliff at one point, pointed to the sky, and said, "I think we might need to take cover because this looks like a pretty big storm." Cliff rolled his eyes and said, "Naw, let's keep going for a little longer." And he took off heading west. I was a little ticked that he hadn't listened to me, but as the older guy on this small team, I decided it best to go along and at least be there in case something happened to either of us. Moving forward also helped us be that much further ahead for tomorrow's work.

Cliff and I had made it maybe a few more yards when suddenly, there was a flash of lightning followed by an immediate crash of thunder that shook the ground where we stood. The wind began gusting, and I could hear tree limbs cracking with so many leaves blowing off the trees that it looked like a yellow and green downpour. It felt like we were in the middle of a hurricane or tornado. Cliff took off running to find cover. I yelled at him to slow down and stop running. I don't think Cliff was panicked, but he felt terrible because he misjudged the storm event and wanted to find cover.

As the wind intensity increased, suddenly, it began raining and raining hard. I stopped near a pile of fallen trees that had made a rough canopy or roof. I yelled to Cliff to stop running and return, but he was gone. I cried Cliff's name several times. The wind was whipping leaves and debris, and I finally squatted under the makeshift canopy and decided I'd have to ride this one out. I told myself Cliff was old enough that he should have some sense and would seek cover until this thing was over.

I tried using my radio to see if I could contact Cliff, but all I got was static.

The wind and rain were intense. To add to this, the occasional flash of lightning or bang of thunder just added to the excitement of the event. I hoped Cliff had enough sense to be safe.

The last I saw before hunkering under the fallen logs was Cliff running toward a thick grove of trees. I hoped there was a canopy that could keep some of the rain off if he made it there.

As the rain began to soak everything, I was thankful that this little pile of logs seemed dry. At least it is drier than being out in the middle of this storm. I settled in and hoped this was a short storm.

Chapter Nine

Roger and I were busy following the orders given to us by our illustrious leader, Tom. NO, I don't dislike Tom. I think, for me, it's just that I don't like being told what to do. Yeah, I know I've been told that one of these days, I'll be put in my place and understand and accept that place as my predestination. But until then, I planned to buck the system every chance I got. I think that's why I liked playing pranks on people. It was a way of breaking the rules and social traditions by cutting up, being funny, and acting silly.

As we were following "orders" and Roger and I were chopping a path through the brush, Roger mentioned that the sky in the West was starting to look dark and ominous. He suggested that maybe we consider finding some coverage or protection. He said he was concerned we hadn't reviewed the weather maps before we began today's work but figured the storm would blow over if we found a place to rest for a minute.

Of course, I didn't agree with him, so when we were suddenly inundated with lightning, winds, thunder, and what seemed like an apocalyptic rainstorm, I took off running west and told Roger we could still make some headway before the storm broke.

I was wrong.

As I commented, the rain and wind suddenly were so intense that I lost sight of Roger. I saw a small grove of low-lying trees and scrub brush nearby and took off running, hoping I wouldn't get struck by lightning. I thought I heard Roger yelling to stop running, but with the crazy weather hitting us, all I could think of was to run and find shelter. I'm glad I was a good runner in school. Making good time, I quickly hunkered down in the little thicket of trees. The canopy of thick tree limbs and leaves was so dense that it kept the bulk of this rainstorm's precipitation away from me. I was shocked at just how dry this little natural space was.

As I listened to the rain slapping the leaves above me, I tried glancing out of my little sanctuary to see if I could locate Roger. I didn't see him anywhere. The storm was intensifying. It grew darker; the lightning flashed, and the thunder boomed. I just leaned back inside the little area I had found, hunkered down, and decided to wait.

I no sooner squatted back down before remembering we were carrying radios and pulled out my radio to try and radio Roger. I got static. I tried sending a message but was still waiting for a response that didn't seem to be coming anytime soon. '*Damn it,*' I thought. '*What good is technology when it doesn't work when you need it the most?*' I checked my cell phone, and nope, just as warned, there was no signal.

I decided it was best to sit still and ride out this storm. As with most storms in Florida, they would blow up out of nowhere and threaten you within an inch of your life, and minutes later, the sun would be out, the birds would be chirping, and you'd instantly forget you had just experienced a thrashing storm, well, except for the steam rising off of the ground and pavement. Whoever thinks Florida is paradise needs to lay off the drugs and booze because Florida's weather can be nothing but sheer hell.

I truly hoped Roger was safe and would search for him just as soon as this monsoon stopped.

As I was sitting in my little cocoon, I glanced around. I looked again in Roger's direction and suddenly noticed a broken-down fence running northerly. I may not be the brightest light in the room, but I realized that I must have run over our property line when I was running to seek shelter from the storm. I probably hadn't even noticed the fence since most of it was lying on the ground. Of course, I didn't get out and look at that fence connection to see if there were any survey markers. I will do that after this storm breaks while trying to find Roger.

I didn't think anything more of it. I was wearing the company uniform, so if I came across anyone, I could provide information so they wouldn't shoot me as a trespasser. I decided that as soon as the storm passed, I would return to that property line just to be safe. Generally, if you are caught trespassing, you are reprimanded and can be fined or jailed, but there are crazies out here who prefer to shoot first and then ask questions. I didn't feel like running into anyone with a gun.

The storm continued to pound the area we were in. As I took inventory of the little place where I had found shelter, I noted another canopy of trees next to mine. It looked thicker and drier on the ground. I decided I would run over there and hunker again. The less wet I am, the better off I am.

I jumped up and ran a few quick trots over to the next tree canopy. I had just reached the densely overgrown area when another blinding flash of lightning hit. This time, the thunder wasn't immediate. To me, this meant the storm was rapidly moving away from us, as there was a delay from lightning strikes to thunder events. I thought, 'Well, that's reassuring.'

As I stepped under the new canopy of trees, the next thing I remember was the feeling of being pulled up into a ball and lifted off the ground. This happened so fast that I was initially confused and disoriented. I was shocked, and I yelled, "WHAT THE FUCK!!!"

I stopped struggling and took inventory of what had happened. I realized I had stepped on what appeared to be a booby trap like you'd see in old war movies. I was hanging about fifteen feet off of the ground and swinging. I reached for my backpack and machete and remembered I had taken them off at the previous canopy of trees and had dropped them as I entered this drier area. So, unfortunately, that meant my knives, machete, and radio were on the ground, somewhere fifteen feet below.

My heart was racing. I thought, '*What the fuck did I just step into?' This was so unusual.*' I do go hunting from time to time, so I thought maybe this could have something to do with hunting, but I still felt uneasy about this, and of course, now I was captured and couldn't even get hold of anyone. I decided the best thing to do would be just to remain calm, and as soon as the storm passed, Roger would find me and cut me down, and we could both have a long laugh about it, that is, as we were racing to get off of this fucking crazy piece of land. The only other thought running through my mind was that this was a better outcome for trespassing than just being shot. However, I wouldn't say I liked either scenario.

Chapter Ten

Morning arrived at Pete and Marcus's camp. Sadly, they had both fallen asleep in their camp chairs before the fire, as it died early in the morning. Unfortunately for the brothers, sleeping in a chair is not the best thing for the human body, so needless to say, both of them were stiff and sore.

As the sky began to lighten, Pete awoke first. He was having some strange dream. He was in a group of men, and they were hooting and hollering as one of the group members was fucking another one on the ground. The strangest thing was that there were no women in his dream. It was men having sex with other men. When Pete woke, he realized his left nipple still itched and was a little puffy. He brushed it with his thumb and forefinger. It itched, but when he thumbed his nipple a few more times, he was amazed that his dick became rock hard. His dick was so hard it was throbbing in his jeans. 'That's got to be a piss hardon,' Pete thought.

He got up and headed to his favorite piss spot. He opened his jeans and hauled out his throbbing cock. He thought, *'Great, I'll never be able to piss with this hardon.'* But sure enough, just as he thought, the piss began to flow. It was a hard, strong stream of fluid. Pete could feel the tension in his loins slowly wane. But he noticed that his hardon wasn't going down at all. The entire time he stood pissing, he was absentmindedly rubbing his left nipple, which was now throbbing and itching, but more of a sensual itch rather than something from a bug bite. As Pete glanced up into the forest, he gently flicked his swollen nipple under his shirt. He finished pissing and slowly stroked his cock to get the last drips of piss out of the slit, but his cock remained hard, and he was now absentmindedly rubbing and flicking his nipple with his left hand and began stroking his cock with his right hand.

Pete finally awoke from his sensual stupor and thought, *'What the fuck is wrong with me? I never stroke my cock. And my nipples have never been sensitive.'* He even tried an experiment. He flicked his right nipple, and nothing happened. But when he would return to his left nipple and flick it, waves of sizzling sexual heat coursed through his body. He shuddered, stopped stroking/flicking, and said, "Damn, something isn't right here."

Pete forced himself to stop this "self-play" and headed back toward the still and campsite. When he returned to the now-dead campfire, he noted Marcus was gone. He figured Marcus must have gotten up and gone for his morning piss. Pete decided to make some coffee and grab a quick bite.

The brothers were going to have another busy day. They needed to finish the cook by allowing it to cool so they could place the newly developed "drink" into jars to set aside for fermenting. Once this task was completed, they would need to tear down the still and configure everything to install the new tank that Pete had been able to acquire quickly through the various connections he had.

Although Pete was confident the location of his still was safe, he thought it a good idea to completely tear down the still and move it to a new location nearby to keep his tracks hidden. All the time he'd been cooking in this area, he had never had any issues with law enforcement or others trying to break in and steal his products. But it was a good idea occasionally to move everything and set up a new shop, and since this failing tank needed to be replaced anyway, now was the time to pick up and move everything.

Pete was still annoyed by his rock-hard cock. Every movement in his jeans was almost torment. He wanted to get off badly, which was not like him. As he kept groping his crotch and squeezing, he thought, '*Where the hell is Marcus?*'

Just about that time, Marcus came walking out of the wooded area. He was yawning, but the thing that Pete noticed more was the huge bulge in his shorts. Pete and Marcus had occasionally seen one another's junk and made no issues of it. Pete noticed that Marcus's nipples were turning into hard buttons under his shirt. But it was back to the enormous bulge swinging in Marcus's shorts as he returned to camp that held Pete's attention.

As Marcus sauntered into camp, still yawning, he reached down, grabbed his crotch, squeezed it hard, and said, "Damn, I cannot get this hardon to go away." Pete rolled his eyes, and Marcus said, "Sorry, I didn't mean for that to sound nasty, but damn, I just don't know what's happening." Pete decided he'd keep his sexual issues to himself, which meant he would have to stop grabbing and squeezing his crotch, at least while in Marcus's presence. You know, being the older brother, he felt he needed to be the responsible one, even if not touching his constantly hard cock would be a difficult task to complete.

The brothers sipped coffee and slowly talked through what they needed to get done for the day. After a few minutes, Pete got up and checked the status of the still. It felt as if the fluid was cooled enough to start transferring the new moonshine into the jars they had stacked and ready to go. Once the jars were filled and stacked into Marcus's truck and safely covered with tarps to camouflage everything, those jars could sit in the truck the rest of the day and continue to ferment. This would give the brothers plenty of time to dismantle the still, replace failed parts, and set up and prepare for another new cook in a few days. Pete wanted to return to production as soon as possible, considering everyone seemed to enjoy his shine these days. Having a still sit idle is not making him any money.

They settled into a routine of filling every jar, capping it, and placing it in Marcus's truck. After about 2 hours of draining, loading, capping, and transporting to their vehicle, they could pronounce this batch of shine as "finished." Again, Pete missed that this batch was also short several pints from the average volume he would produce due to the leaky cook tank.

Now came the time for the great "breakdown" of the current still. Pete had already scoped out a new location just over the hill from this one and in an even more secluded area. This meant no time would be wasted trying to find a decent site, as Pete had already done this preliminary investigative research. Connections were pulled apart. Racks and tables were disconnected. Everything was ready to be transported over the hill.

Pete and Marcus had both been working like dogs all morning. The day was sunny but just as humid as any other day. By noon, both brothers were drenched in sweat. The entire crotch of Pete's jeans was damp. His shirt clung to his body. He was thinking of just taking off his shirt, as it was beginning to be weighed down by his sweat, and that was just more weight to carry around while doing all of this manual labor. Marcus was just as wet, if not wetter, than

Pete. Marcus's shirt and shorts were both completely drenched in sweat. Marcus finally removed his shirt to stay a bit cooler as they worked to get everything moved, and they began to reinstall all of the pieces in the new location.

As they began putting all of the parts of the still back into position in their new location, Pete finally broke down and took off his shirt. He wiped his swarthy, hairy, sweat-soaked chest with his shirt and threw it at Marcus. Being the instinctual athlete, Marcus caught the shirt like a football, and before either he or Pete was even aware, Marcus shoved the wet and sweaty shirt under his nose and took a deep breath. As he breathed in, Pete could see Marcus's stiff cock seem to get even harder, and it even looked like it bounced inside of his jock and gym shorts.

Pete scratched his head and looked at Marcus strangely. Marcus suddenly realized what he was doing and threw Pete's shirt near the campfire. They made eye contact, but neither brother had any expression on their face. They held one another in a blank yet impenetrable stare.

Pete's damned left nipple suddenly itched again, and he absentmindedly rubbed it. When he did, he suddenly felt his stiff cock grow even harder. If he pushed his Kegel muscle internally, this caused the front of his jeans to move in and out, almost as if his crotch was breathing and would shoot waves of heat and electricity through his groin, almost as if he'd been hit with a molten cannonball that had gone all the way through him, burned everything, and was coming back for a second pass. It was a "good" burn, not a painful one. He looked up and saw Marcus staring at the throbbing bulge in his jeans. Marcus suddenly looked up and caught Pete staring at him.

They stared for a few seconds, and then the gaze was broken; they each cleared their throats, spat on the ground, grabbed their hard crotches as if to scratch them, like some guys do absentmindedly, and continued working to reassemble the still.

Was this strange? Yes, it was. The brothers were deep in personal thought, trying to understand or decipher what was happening.

Pete and Marcus were putting the last fittings together on their new still. Pete stepped back and took stock of what they had accomplished. Granted, Pete had been doing this "tear down and rebuild" process for quite some time, but with Marcus's assistance, things worked out even more smoothly and went much faster.

Pete stood looking at the new setup and just admired their work. Marcus strolled over and stood next to him. Pete placed his arm around his little brother's back, and Marcus threw his arm over his big brother's shoulders. They stood reviewing their work, and both seemed to lean into one another. They could feel their sweaty torsos sticking together as they bent and breathed.

Pete suddenly noticed the strong, musky smells wafting from Marcus's hairy armpits. Again, without warning, Pete's semi-hard dick jumped to attention. He caught himself breathing deeply to get as much of that manly scent into his lungs as possible. He tightened his grip on his arm, wrapped it around Marcus's waist, and pulled Marcus closer.

Pete's head was spinning. He felt like he was floating in some electrostatic mist. His entire body felt tingly. He realized his nipples were hard and looked like those pink pencil erasers you used to have in elementary school. They seemed so sensitive. Even the slightest breath of wind made them feel like they were on fire, but that fire kept shooting pulses straight to his dick.

Marcus could feel Pete tighten his grip along his waist. He responded by reaching further over Pete's shoulder with his arm. This caused Marcus's armpit to spread further, releasing even more of his sweaty scent into the air. He could feel Pete breathing heavily. He could also feel his and Pete's sweat blending along the areas where the brothers' bodies touched, and the sweat dripped and ran down their shiny muscles.

As they leaned into one another, Pete glanced up at the sky and suddenly realized it was darkening. He then seemed to notice the wind beginning to pick up. Pete caught Marcus looking at him. As Pete glanced into Marcus's eyes, waves of hot, sizzling electricity raced through Pete's body. Pete was enjoying the heat emanating from Marcus's body; strangely, he didn't want that feeling to end.

As both brothers looked back at the product of their hard work, there was a flash of lightning and an immediate crash of thunder. The brothers jumped and suddenly realized the storm was upon them. Having spent more time in this area, Pete was aware of a grove of trees just a few hundred yards from this new still site. The only thing Pete would need to caution Marcus about was that he had set a netted booby trap a while back. So, once they raced to the grove of trees, Pete would need to warn Marcus of the trap's location so they could weather the storm, and Pete could explain why he's the more mentally fucked up brother for even installing such a thing. Or at least that's what Pete thought Marcus would think.

Pete broke the brother's embrace and said, "We need to take cover. Heading to that tree stand is quicker than getting to our trucks. I think this storm is getting ready to break open."

Just as Pete finished his sentence, there was another blinding flash of lightning, followed immediately by an earth-shattering bang of thunder, and then the winds started picking up.

Pete grabbed Marcus's arm and ran toward the little tree grove. As they raced toward the forest, the wind continued to whip leaves and rain into their faces. There was another flash of lightning, but the thunder didn't come immediately, which told the brothers that this storm was rapidly passing through and already beginning to move away from them.

Just as the ground shook from another roll of thunder, they made it to the trees. As they stepped under the canopy, Pete threw his arm across Marcus's chest, like a mother would do if she made an emergency stop and her child was in the front seat but not strapped in safely. You know that reflex occurs even if you are strapped in. It's just human nature.

As their eyes adjusted to the darkness under the canopy of trees, Marcus suddenly noticed what looked like an army camouflage netting material hanging and swinging from one of the trees. The brothers stepped into the canopy, and someone in the netting yelled, "Hey, Help me, please. I don't know what happened, but I am trapped."

Pete looked at Marcus, and they looked over at the figure swinging from the trees. They looked down at one another's crotches and noticed they were both hard. The mound in Marcus's jock and gym shorts was prominent. It looked like he was carrying a sledgehammer in his pants. Pete's jeans were bulging so thickly that it almost appeared like the buttons at his crotch would explode and turn into miniature missiles once his dick crashed through the opening.

The storm outside this treed area continued to rage but rapidly moved out of the site. Rumbles of thunder could be heard in the distance, and a quick flash of lightning lit up in the sky occasionally, but everything seemed to settle down.

Pete glanced up at the swinging victim and yelled, "Now, what the hell is a guy like you doing in a place like this, and how did you get into this predicament?"

Of course, it was Cliff who was swinging from the trees. He heard Pete asking this random and honestly stupid question.

Cliff yelled, "Dude, I work for a land survey team. We got caught in this crazy storm, and I ran over here to get out of the rain, and someone has set a trap here. Please, can you get me down from here?"

Pete grinned at his brother and looked up at the netting again. This was becoming a fun game. He looked up at Cliff and said, "You realize you're trespassing on private property, don't cha, boy?" Pete said this, even though he well knew that he, his brother, and this new captive were all trespassing, but it sounded more official and gave Pete the upper hand for negotiating purposes, should that become necessary. Again, Pete agreed with the rest of his family; this was still their land, and they were loaning it to the government for an easement. That misaligned belief did help give Pete an authoritative tone, which helped him dominate this entire interaction.

Cliff yelled, "Yes, I realize I went over the wrong property line as I ran for cover from this storm. I apologize, but if you just cut me down, I'll grab my survey equipment and head back over to the correct side of the property, no questions asked."

Pete looked at his little brother, musclebound and sweating, and his cock jerked again. Pete thought, '*Why the hell does it feel so freaking good to look at, feel, and smell my brother?*'

As Pete glanced at Marcus, Marcus came back to Pete's side and placed his arm around Pete's waist this time. Marcus groped the massive mound in his gym shorts and glanced at the swinging net.

Marcus said, "Um, I understand mistakes happen, but you can't just waltz onto our property and expect us to let you go because you say you're sorry." He glanced in Pete's direction, looking for approval from his big brother to prove he was an active and supportive part of this family and supported the belief that they still owned this land and could lay claim to it whenever necessary. It was Marcus's way of sharing, with Pete, all responsibility for this land and its management. After all, family is always thicker than water. Pete grinned back at his brother for first showing his loyalty to the family, even if both brothers' beliefs were misguided.

Cliff needed clarification. He said, "What? I need to get down, and I'll get back to my team over on our side of the property." He said, "I have paperwork and am wearing a company uniform. If you get me down from here, I can prove who I am and why I'm here."

Marcus grinned and said, "OK, no problem. We will get you down, but before we get you back to your people, let's check to ensure you haven't broken anything.

Marcus's brain was slowly but surely twisting as he succumbed to whatever strange venom those danged mosquitoes had injected. He began formulating a plan. An evil grin appeared as he gently and methodically said to Pete, "Hey, hang tight for just a couple minutes and watch our captive."

Pete, usually the dominant force between the brothers, was so foggy-brained that he just nodded and kept staring up at their new captive, hanging and wiggling in the trees. Marcus jogged back over to the still and reached for his backpack. He decided this to be an excellent time to try out some of those strange pills that that new girl he recently fucked, had given him. Something in his throbbing cock wanted to see if having someone take these pills would make them take orders from someone else and not question it or render them helpless so he could control them. Maybe Marcus was tired of being the little brother, and it was time to take charge. Hell, all he wanted to do was try anything to relieve the pressure in his pants.

Pete placed a thumb into the waist of his jeans and allowed his fingers to hang down over his throbbing crotch. He tilted his hips, and absent-mindedly mumbled to Marcus, "OK, do what you need to do, and I'll watch our little swinging prize here."

Neither brother was aware of what was happening. Their libido and sexual orientation mechanisms had converted from straight thoughts and actions to gay ones because of the bites they had received. The infection worked subtly, but unlike a typical mosquito bite, when these bugs wanted to feed, they injected a tainted venom that numbs the skin but then works against a regular male sex drive, both increasing the male species' attraction to other males, less to females, and the almost painfully intense drive to procreate, not with women, but with this new-found object of their attentions, men. The effect was reminiscent of hunting-gathering societies of the past, again minus the female species. When bitten, men who naturally possessed a more masculine attitude or nature tended to become enraged hunters, hunting for one sexual experience after another, just like their forefathers would have hunted wild beasts for sustenance. This strange infection the brothers were fighting caused men who naturally had lower testosterone levels to be less dominant, acting, and non-aggressive and tended to retreat, allowing the more alpha male presence to control the situation.

Pete and Marcus's overnight interest in masculine men with muscles and hairy bodies, sweat, musky body odors, spit and piss, among other things, seemed completely normal. Their brain and sexual desires were altered to seek out the strongest and most virile of their species to procreate by injecting their infected sperm in any opening they could get to on their prey.

Nasty, lustful thoughts of deep sexual pleasures to be had assaulting those they hunted and captured seemed just as natural, to them, as the sun rising and setting and that green fog puffing through the trees. At least that's what the brothers' skeeter-infested brains had convinced them.

When he returned to the new still's location, Marcus grabbed a water bottle. He cracked the lid and inserted two of the pills as he'd been instructed by the girl who shared them with him. While he was doing this, his eyes lit up, and he added a blue pill of Viagra to the mix and shook the bottle again. He had stolen the Viagra from one of his friend's dad's medicine cabinets. He figured that since his friend's mom was pretty ugly, his dad didn't need to get hard and have sex all the time so that he wouldn't miss a few pills, and the world would be saved from the creation of another ugly child.

As he watched the pills dissolve clearly into the water bottle, Marcus thought, '*Yeah, this girl I met is a walking talking medicine cabinet, but she was a great fuck, so you just couldn't discount that. However, fucking her dad or brother would be even hotter.*' Marcus looked at the bottle, stopped shaking it, and seemed to think deeply, '*I'd rather fuck her dad than her? Yeah, fuck right. I'd rather rape her father and brother raw and rude before touching her wet, smelly pussy.*'

Marcus placed the bottle he made for his captive into the back pocket of his sweaty shorts. This caused his shorts to pull down and hang low along his hips. His shorts this low suddenly brought into view the impressive, chiseled ridge from each of his hips and formed a "V" as it aimed straight for the central connection where his massive, manly, uncut tool hung. Marcus was hot and sweaty. The infection was causing his entire body to sizzle, so pulling the shorts down helped make him feel more relaxed, toned down the waves of electricity shooting through his body, and just showed off all the hard work he'd put in at the gym over his lifetime.

Marcus chuckled as his infected brain continued conjuring more intense sexual ideas. He grabbed two more bottles of water, snapped the tops, dropped a Viagra in each, closed them up, and shook them well.

The storm had finally dissipated, and there was just a breeze slowly dying down but still strong enough to rustle the leaves here and there. The clouds were still heavy and dark, and you could occasionally hear thunder in the distance.

As Marcus walked back to the grove of trees with water and his trusty hunting knife, his dick throbbed inside the jock strap under his shorts. He kept grabbing and slapping his bulge as he made his return. Marcus thought, '*Damn, it feels good to slap and punch my cock. Fucking driving me nuts.*' Marcus felt hot, flustered, excited, and horny. He started holding his and his brother's water bottles near his crotch, which caused them to bang against his shorts and jock with every step. Occasionally, one or both bottles would slam into Marcus's balls and send a numbing shockwave through his groin and down his legs, but with his infected mental state, Marcus relished every painful slam.

Marcus got back to the trees and walked over to the hanging net. He grabbed the water bottle from his back pocket and reached up as high as his thick arms would go, saying, "Hey, here's some water. My brother and I will try to get you down; hang in there for a few minutes."

Cliff reached down, took the bottle, and said, "Thanks, man, I truly appreciate your help."

Cliff removed the lid of the bottled water and guzzled the liquid inside. He was sort of in shock and hadn't even noticed the typical clicking sound of a fresh bottle of water when you twist the lid and break the seal for the first time. Cliff was thirsty, angry, felt like a fool for getting into this mess, and just wanted this mess to be over.

As Marcus returned to Pete, he handed him one of the other two bottles he had brought. He softly told Pete he had laced the water in their captive's bottle and wanted to see what would happen. In a few minutes, they would see if there was a reaction and decide if/when to bring down their new prisoner. Marcus and Pete guzzled their water as well. The storm was almost gone, and the steamy heat of the wetlands was beginning to return in full force.

Marcus grinned but didn't tell Pete he had also laced their waters with Viagra. As he shook his head, he thought, *'Some secrets are better kept to oneself.'* While this thought occurred, his dick throbbed inside his jock strap again.

Marcus could feel the inside of his jock getting moist and sticky, and he knew it wasn't the sweat he was feeling. His throbbing cock was spewing clear drops and strands of precum and coating the inside of his jock. His hard uncut cock was pushing the fabric of his jockstrap, causing his cock to bend ever so slightly, sort of like an I-Beam on a building that is overstressed and is bending in the middle. This pulled the foreskin that hung over the head of his cock down enough to allow his piss slit to rub against the jock strap, which added more stickiness to the mix. Marcus's piss slit dribbled gush after gush of thick salty precum; the feeling of his cock rubbing against the moist, sticky, rough fabric of his jock caused the fire in his loins to go into afterburner mode.

Right away, after Cliff guzzled the water he'd been given, he noticed his vision blur. He jerked inside of the netting where he was still hanging and said with slurred speech, "What tha hell, man? Did you do something to the-tha-that water? Cliff struggled several times, and you could suddenly hear him breathing heavily. Cliff had passed out.

Cliff's body went limp, and the empty water bottle slipped from his hand, fell through an opening in the netting, and bounced onto the ground. Marcus slapped Pete on the ass, flashed a twisted smile, ran over to where the release rope was held, untied the knots, and slowly allowed the netting to glide to the forest floor below. Cliff and the camouflage netting basket he'd been hanging in rested on the spongy ground. Cliff had passed out, and it looked like he was taking an afternoon nap to any passersby.

Marcus and Pete walked over and looked down at Cliff. Cliff was breathing deeply while on his drugged-up journey. Marcus looked at Pete and said, "We need to get him back to our camp and tie him up until we can figure out what we will do with him.

Marcus continued, "I mean, he said something about his team. And he is way too close to our stuff for anyone else to come loping into camp by surprise, right?"

Pete was still foggy because even though what Marcus said to him seemed normal, a tiny voice said this plan was incorrect. As Pete's mind became even fuzzier from the effects of the mosquito bite on his nipple, he didn't even feel like fighting Marcus and went along with whatever Marcus had in mind. He nodded lamely and said, "OK, you got it, man."

Marcus pointed to the backpack and radio at the furthest edge of the grove of trees, glanced at Pete, grabbed the younger Cliff and lifted him like the rag doll he still was, threw him over his shoulder in a fireman's carry position, slapped Pete's hard ass in his jeans and said, "Get that stuff over there and bring along the rope that was attached to that netting, Big Brother," and headed back over the hill toward the still and their newly set up campsite.

As Pete followed along, he kept watching Marcus's ass muscles flex with every step as the brothers returned to their camp, and Marcus carried their captive over his shoulder like nothing more than a sack of potatoes. Pete also stared longingly, while licking his lips, at the strapping young buck of a man hanging over his little brother's thick shoulders.

Pete didn't understand why, but along their short journey, every step he took or even the slightest breeze against his left nipple would shoot jets of electricity into his throbbing cock. When he thought his cock couldn't get any more rigid, he was surprised repeatedly because it just kept feeling like it grew harder and harder. Walking in his jeans was becoming increasingly painful as you could see the hard cock forming a log in the crotch. Each step Pete took would brush up against that log and force it to move up and down, almost as if the crotch of his jeans was stroking his impressive cock back and forth and up and down.

Pete's dick was doing summersaults as he felt his throbbing nipple, but he also noticed that each time his younger brother took a step along their path, when Marcus's hairy muscled legs moved, and his muscled ass would bulge as it flexed, that Pete's dick also throbbed and swelled. Pete was in a state of confusion. He had never had any attraction to his brother that way. Pete thought, '*Heck, I've never had any thoughts or attraction for any man because I'm not gay.*' He thought to himself as he now began to take notice of Cliff's appearance and, once again, each time he glanced at Cliff's body, he caught himself taking in a deep breath, breathing out, and feeling like all he wanted to do was rip his dick out of his pants and beat himself into an orgasmic explosion. He shook his head as if someone was trying to shake the water out of their ears and followed Marcus as their new moonshine masterpiece came into view.

Marcus continued with their captive as the brothers returned to their camp. He dropped Cliff from his shoulder and walked to a giant older tree near the center. Marcus looked at the tree and noted how its trunk leaned toward a bit of clearing just to the side of the new still. The tree trunk was stout, which could hold several captive men's weight if needed. Marcus chuckled at that thought, and his dick jerked and gushed a nice load of precum into his jock as he pictured several men tied up, writhing, and unable to do anything but accept their new sexual fate.

Marcus shook his head for a minute, then instructed Pete to grab the ropes and get the rachet-styled tie-down ropes they kept for transporting "delicate" merchandise to and from their customers.

Seeming to have lost all will, Pete nodded in Marcus's direction, took off to the truck to grab the additional ropes, and headed back to the campsite. Once there, Marcus forced Cliff's limp body into position and instructed Pete to help tie their new captive to the tree.

Marcus had been a Boy Scout for a couple of years when he was younger and had learned several rope and knot types. Pete had thought getting Marcus involved in Scouts was something he could do for Marcus that couldn't be done by their father, but Marcus had quickly grown bored with all of the challenges the Scouts required, so his stint with the group was short but long enough for him to gain some valuable knowledge. You know, like how to tie knots to tie up a prisoner, if necessary. Kids can learn the darndest things.

As Pete stood almost like a zombie, Marcus held Cliff against the tree and instructed him to tie ropes and binds to hold Cliff in a roped position. Marcus's evil mind followed a process of wrapping cords around Cliff's body and the tree. Marcus helped Pete tie Cliff so that his entire body was immobilized, but he was hanging from several ropes tethered to the tree's overhanging trunk. This effectively allowed Cliff's body to be swung into any position desired without having to untie or retie knots. Imagine the string on a large musical harp, loose enough to flick it, and it will wobble. If the brothers wanted to have fun, they could push Cliff's body in a circular motion, and he would swing from one brother to the other.

To anyone standing by, Cliff's body looked like a side of beef hanging from the tree, just like sides of meat would hang in a cooler at a butcher shop or just like you'd find if you came across a deer hunter gutting his prey in the woods.

As they finished their knot-tying, Marcus and Pete breathed heavily. With their willpower continually diminishing and sexual focus strengthening, the brothers paused to touch, caress, and pat one another's bodies, sometimes a caress on a tight ass, another time a bump of crotches. It was all about body contact.

The brothers stepped back to admire their work. Marcus stood with his legs spread apart, allowing the breeze to cool his throbbing groin. Pete stepped next to his little brother, raised his arm, laid it over Marcus's shoulder, and bent at the elbow to place a couple of fingers to his mouth.

Marcus got a whiff of Pete's sweaty pit, and again, his dick thrust forward and caused his jock to shake, jiggling his ball sack in the process. It felt like jingle bells at Christmas time.

Pete and Marcus wiped the drool from the sides of their mouths at the site of Cliff hanging here in their camp.

"When this dude comes to, he's gonna awake to a big surprise," said Pete, as he chuckled deeply.

Marcus glanced at his brother, reached behind, smacked his ass hard, winked, and laughed, "I think he's gonna like this surprise. And if he doesn't, I know we will."

Cliff was helplessly tied, with his back positioned to make his body arch forward, with ropes running across his chest, around his thighs, and up and around his groin and ass.

There were ropes around the tops of Cliff's lace-up work boots. Those ropes pulled Cliff's ankles up toward his buttocks. This position caused Cliff's knees to spread wide and exposed the prominent bulge in Cliff's work shorts. His ass was also exposed where his legs were pulled apart. Cliff's hands were tied behind his back at the wrists to the same ropes that bound his ankles toward his ass. He looked like a butterfly cocoon without the cocoon.

Marcus and Pete patted and caressed one another's wet, muscled bodies as they slowly circled the tree where Cliff was hanging. They would frequently move closer to their victim, sometimes wiping sweat off his brow or other exposed portions of his body and licking their wet hands while admiring Cliff's bitter, moist taste or taking a deep whiff of Cliff's sweat-stained armpits.

Pete and Marcus had removed their shirts earlier in the day while working on the still. The intense Florida humidity kicked back into high gear as the storm passed, and a little sun began to pop around the clouds.

Rivulets of sweat washed down their chests and muscled torsos. The sweat would pool here and there on Pete's chest because of the mass of hair that would trap that moisture. Occasionally, Pete would absentmindedly run his fingers through the thick, wet matting of fur on his large pecs, take his wet fingers, and run them along Cliff's pink and pouty lips. He was still knocked out, so he had no idea his body was the focus of attention for the two raging men.

Marcus was also sweating, but because he wasn't as hairy as Pete, the sweat ran more quickly down his torso, causing his gym shorts to grow wetter and wetter. Marcus placed his hands inside the waistband of his shorts and gently caressed his sticky jockstrap. He pulled his fingers out of his shorts, put them to his nose, sniffed and licked them, and then ran his precum-coated fingers along Cliff's mouth, mixing his precum with his older brother's spit.

As they continued to admire their ropework, Cliff was hung motionless, head pulled back by a rope around his chin. Cliff's mouth was hanging open. The brothers were already prepared to gag him if, when he awakens, he decides to be stupid and start yelling. They had brought duct tape from Marcus's truck.

As the brothers admired their work, they heard that strange screeching sound again. The hum was weird because it came and went like sometimes, you'd listen to something, but then you wouldn't, and your brain and ears were left wondering if you heard something or were only dreaming. This time Pete felt a sting on his right ass cheek, and Marcus felt a bite on his right nipple. The brothers jumped, slapped their prospective bite areas, and shouted because the sting was so damned intense.

After jumping around for a few minutes, both brothers' bodies feeling like they'd been dipped in molten lava, they calmed enough to refocus their minds on their new captive. Their brains were still fogged over, and they were not thinking logically, but at least they weren't hopping around like crazed animals.

Pete yelled, "Them Goddamned KWEER SKEETERS." He said in his Southern drawl, "What the hell is wrong with them, and why won't they leave us alone?"

As Pete yelled, Marcus felt waves of heat flashing through his body, his dick throbbing and his ass muscles flexing repeatedly. Marcus had this uncontrollable urge to want to kiss someone. While Marcus tried to understand his strange feelings, Pete hopped over, hugged him, and said, "Damned Skeeters are gonna be my death." No sooner had he said that than Marcus returned the bear hug. Both men stood face to face, arms wrapped around one another, sweaty, hairy, and muscled chests heaving and brushing one another. Marcus's and Pete's eyes locked. They stared. Their heads slowly began to move toward one another. The brothers' mouths were ajar. Their tongues moved gently back and forth along their lower lips inside their mouths.

Marcus grabbed the back of Pete's neck. At first, Pete looked deeply into Marcus's eyes and attempted to pull away, only to note Marcus's massive bicep flex as he put more pressure on his hold and began pulling Pete's face closer to his.

Pete returned the favor and clasped his hand behind Marcus's neck. Marcus didn't pull away like Pete had. They stared at one another as if there was nothing else to look at on this planet. As Marcus pulled Pete toward him, Pete's arm flexed, and both brothers' heads began to shake as they strained to stop the inevitable. Some part of their former selves was trying to fight this urge to kiss, but they were losing their battle.

Their faces were ever closer, their heads shaking; Marcus's thick lips finally brushed against Pete's scruffy bearded face. Marcus felt thousands of hot needles stinging his face and lips as Pete's stubble brushed against him.

Marcus's dick visibly jumped in his shorts. Pete attempted to pull away yet again. He had a strained look that said he was confused, but Marcus's grasp was intense and unbreakable.

The brothers leaned closer to one another. And suddenly, their faces were so close that their lips brushed one another. As if magnets had been used, their bodies quickly blended, and they grasped one another and pulled each other closer and closer. Their mouths were finally locked. Lips connected, and suddenly, another mass rush of heat crashed over them, and they began devouring each other, almost like wild animals would eat a raw piece of meat. That frenzy is natural and uninhibited.

Pete's tongue was fighting with Marcus's mouth. Marcus held Pete in such a tight hug that Pete almost couldn't breathe. Sweat was flying off of their hair, chests, arms and running down their legs. The brothers continued kissing and hugging, and their arms and hands began to explore one another's bodies. They were rubbing their hard chests together, grinding their pants, and causing wet spots to appear on their massive bulges.

Marcus pulled his hand away from Pete's neck, made a fist, and punched Pete's flexing throbbing pecs as the brothers continued their voracious, manly kissing.

Suddenly, as if an alarm had gone off, they pulled apart, wiping their mouths. Pete looked aghast at Marcus. Just as they made eye contact again, they hopped away while smacking various parts of their bodies. They had both been stung again by those damned skeeters.

After a few hops and hollers, the brothers stopped again, looked deeply into each other's eyes, and moved back together. This time, they yanked and tugged at each other's shorts and jeans. Before the brothers were even aware, their mouths were again conjoined, fighting hot, wet battles as tongues and lips swiped and jabbed at one another's mouths. This time, they made no effort to pull apart.

Although the initial bite from the "Kweer Skeeter" might take longer to take control of the victim's libido and brain processes, after the first bite, any additional bites added fuel to the fire and would instantly increase the victim's sex drive. Of course, the victim's metabolism also affected how quickly the mosquitoes' venom got into their system and started working.

Just like a regular mosquito bite, some people are affected by them more than others. A slower metabolism would cause the infection to take longer to infiltrate the blood system, so the effects could appear more slowly. But once bitten, each successive bite would immediately boost the level of infection.

Pete and Marcus were standing in a deep, hard bear hug. They were kissing. Pete's jeans were now falling below his knees. He was standing there in his boxer briefs. Marcus stood proudly as the bulge in his now exposed jockstrap continued to push away from his body so much that you could see his cock, balls, and thick pubes if you looked on either side of the jock. Marcus's jockstrap could not contain his throbbing cock and balls. Marcus's hard cock pushed the fabric of his worn jockstrap to its limits.

As the brothers held their embrace, they began shifting and rubbing their bodies together. Not only were they passing their throbbing cocks back and forth, like a sword fight, but they were also rubbing their legs together. The hair on Pete and Marcus's legs brushed together. Sweat splashed from one brother to the other as they rubbed their bodies.

Marcus grabbed Pete's left nipple and aggressively flicked it with his fingernails. Pete gasped, moaning and gurgling as the brother's mouths reconnected. As tongues continued to fight battle after battle inside their mouths, Pete grabbed Marcus's throbbing cock and squeezed the jockstrap so hard that it made Marcus's knees weak, and he leaned into his brother as their frenzy continued.

Pete then proceeded to flick and twist Marcus's right nipple. The mosquito bite on Marcus's nipple caused it to puff up and become extremely sensitive. As the brothers continued tormenting one another's infected nipples, they kissed, flicked, and twisted until they both began slowly falling to the ground on their knees. By this time, their shorts and pants had been completely removed. Pete and Marcus sat on their knees; chests, waists, thighs, arms, faces, mouths, and lips were all connected as tightly as two humans can connect. Their massive hairy thighs were intertwined to allow them to get even closer to one another.

Marcus and Pete sat in this position, Pete's boxer briefs screaming to be pulled away from his angry cock, and Marcus's dick almost successful at escaping and sliding out the side of his jockstrap. Kneeling before Cliff, the brothers kissed, licked, and continued torturing each other's nipples. Cliff had no idea what was taking place because he was still passed out from the effects of the pills he had been given.

As the brothers continued to lick, touch, caress, and hump one another, Cliff began to regain consciousness. When he realized where he was and realized he was unable to move, he began to jiggle and move his arms and legs, trying to find any way to break free from his bonds. This movement caught Marcus's eye, and he and Pete quickly shifted their focus onto a new subject while staying connected, kissing, licking, and touching.

Chapter Eleven

Cliff awoke in a fog. He quickly realized he had been tied up. He didn't understand why two hairy, muscled, and rough-looking men were half-naked and kissing while kneeling before him. Strangely, Cliff noticed that his dick was hard in his shorts, and all he wanted to do was get off. Of course, maybe because he had recently lost his girlfriend, but even if they were still together, she wouldn't have been here with him on this long project. He hadn't had sex in a while and was thrown off his regular daily routine of jacking off once or twice because he was stuck with his workmates on this job. Still, he could not overlook the insane pulsing feeling inside his cock. He tilted his head left and right and tried to understand why watching two men kissing and making out before him was turning him on so much.

As hot as his skin felt, he was confident that if anyone were to touch him, they would be instantly incinerated. His dick was throbbing and bouncing.

Suddenly, Cliff remembered the water bottle he'd been given and how the drink had caused him to feel strange and finally pass out. He realized he'd been drugged. As quickly as that realization came to him, the drugs in his system pushed those thoughts away, and the focus was, again, on his throbbing cock and how much he felt he needed to get off, no matter who was there to see it.

Cliff started bucking in his restraints, but all he could do was wriggle inside the knotted cocoon the brothers had concocted. He started moaning, trying to formulate words. Speaking seemed virtually impossible. Cliff's entire body was on fire. It felt like a nuclear bomb was going off in his loins, and he didn't care who saw it or shared in that explosion. Come to think of it, he was so horned up that he'd let anyone or anything touch him. Falling in and out of consciousness, Cliff was reeling from the influence of the drugs Marcus had given him.

The Viagra was working, and as Cliff's dick throbbed in his pants and he shook and wiggled to no avail, Cliff saw what he thought was a mosquito, but it was a much larger variety than he'd ever seen. It had some strange green coloring to its body. As he continued watching the mosquito, he suddenly saw two more, then several more. Cliff thought, '*What the fuck?*'

The mosquitoes hovered near Cliff. As Pete and Marcus continued kissing, they slowly shifted closer to Cliff as he hung from the bent and crooked tree. Cliff continued to wriggle his body while hopelessly tied to the ropes. He was secured, and there was nowhere he could go. As he jerked and wriggled in his bindings, he suddenly felt three sharp stabs in his ass and neck from behind. The mosquitoes had stung him. He felt wave after wave of heat thrashing through his body. It felt almost as if the intensity of the earlier feelings he was experiencing had just been turned up 150 percent.

As the "Kweer Skeeter" venom coursed through Cliff's body, he was suddenly aware that all his clothing was burning into his body. Everything touching his body felt unbearably hot and tight. Every square inch of his body was on fire, and the clothing he had on was doing nothing but irritating his skin, causing him to shudder as wave after orgasmic wave coursed through him.

Cliff groaned loudly. The jerking motions he'd been making with his body to try and break free of the ropes holding him became less aggressive and more sensual. Cliff felt wave after wave of heat bursting through his body and continually attacking his groin with hot flashes. The rough texture of the ropes binding him and suspending him freely from the ground was caressing his body in ways he had never felt before. Each movement of his body created a flash of electricity that shot out from the center but then returned like a nuclear explosion to his loins.

Cliff's dick broiled with heat, but it became a sizzling burn, not a fiery one. He opened his eyes wider, panted, moaned again, and tried to formulate words and shout out. He looked down and was speechless as he saw the two hairy, muscular men kneeling before him, kissing and rubbing each other. As he continued watching, the bulge inside his work shorts grew even more prominent. A wet spot began to form just to the left of the zipper of his shorts.

As Cliff continued to swing in torment with his body being attacked by the venom from those weird green pests and watching his captors consume one another in front of him, he started turning and gyrating his body to bend closer to the brothers' faces. By doing this, he could brush his crotch against their faces as they kissed. This movement broke their concentration, and suddenly, they realized Cliff was awake, and he became their newest focus.

Marcus and Pete reached out and grabbed Cliff's swinging body. Cliff tried to pull away because, for one lucid moment, he remembered that men don't hold men like that. But something inside his head dislodged, like a screw working loose on an assembly. His dick jerked and bounced, and he could feel the wetness of precum dripping into his shorts. Like a flash of lightning, Cliff felt explosions and saw stars each time he swung back toward the brothers, and they would kiss and lick as he passed by.

After a few passes like this, Marcus and Pete each latched their hands onto Cliff's muscled ass cheeks as they bounced under his tight-fitting shorts. This caused his cheeks to pull apart, making the seam in the ass of his work shorts stretch tightly from behind. The threads along the back of Cliff's shorts were pulled so tightly that it appeared like his shorts would tear away at that seam. Each time the brothers pulled Cliff's ass cheeks apart, he would feel the air just a little cooler inside his shorts and up along his furry ass crack. Cliff felt intense pressure on his throbbing cock as the crotch of his shorts was pulled tightly over his dick and balls. The tightness of Cliff's throbbing cock and balls being stretched inside his shorts caused Cliff to buck his hips, and that caused Marcus and Pete to ravage one another's mouths even more.

Pete and Marcus pulled against Cliff's ass which caused him to swing toward them. The brothers flexed their arm muscles, stopped Cliff from turning, and held him so his crotch was at their mouths. Both brothers proceeded to lick and spit on Cliff's bulge. Cliff kept telling himself he wasn't gay, but he loved the feeling of their hot mouths on his crotch, causing the front of his shorts to get wetter and wetter with their spit. Of course, it didn't help that Cliff was now suffering effects from the laced water he had drunk and this new infection from those pesky mosquitoes.

As Cliff continued gyrating his body, his crotch would come in contact with one or both brothers. They'd hold him, suck and lick, and then swing him away, with him panting and moaning that he wanted to be turned back to their hot wet mouths.

God damn it, he wanted more.

Chapter Twelve

As the mosquito infection continued to boil Cliff, Pete, and Marcus's blood, they were utterly unaware that just over the hill, they had been discovered, and they were being watched.

As the storm settled, Roger realized he needed to ensure Cliff was okay. The last thing he saw was Cliff running off toward a tree stand just before the storm crashed down upon them. Roger had yelled for Cliff to stop and stay with him, but knowing how bullheaded Cliff can be, he wasn't surprised when Cliff took the initiative to prove his manhood and ran in the opposite direction.

From experience, being out in the weather during a storm isn't always horrible and can be refreshing. The lighting was the part that worried Roger the most, so he was quick to hunker down and stay safe and hoped Cliff had finally made that decision.

As Roger rolled over to start digging out from the area of fallen logs where he had weathered the storm, he rolled against one of the logs poking into the little enclosure he had found. As soon as he felt the prod of the log, he heard a snapping sound. He looked down and realized he had snapped the antenna entirely off of his radio. The connection had broken. That rendered his radio ineffective.

Roger just shook his head, said, "Damnit," and continued to pull himself out of his improvised storm shelter. He brushed himself off. His shorts were stained with mud, and he was a little damp but not soaking wet.

Roger grabbed his backpack, threw the broken parts of his radio in the outer pocket, and headed toward the tree grove where he last saw Cliff. He figured he'd need to be responsible and get Cliff out of any predicament he may have gotten into since he seems to act before thinking a lot of the time.

Roger grinned and shook his head as he walked over to the tree growth and thought, '*Ah, youth. Gone are the days when I take off and try to rule the world without investigating how to do it first.*'

Roger got to the little canopy of trees but didn't see Cliff anywhere. He thought, '*Well, hell, where the heck did Cliff get off to?*' He squatted down and checked the floor area of this little stand of trees. He could see a couple of prints in the damp soil there. The boot prints looked pretty fresh and appeared to be the type of print a hiking or work boot would make. Roger was sure these had to have been made by Cliff.

The area regained its steamy, swampy nature as the sun began to pop in and out of the clouds. Roger could see steam rising off of the ground. He shook his head. As a child, he often thought this steam was the mist from dead people coming out to haunt everyone after a terrible storm.

The only thing this steam rising made Roger think nowadays was how muggy and miserable it would be with all this humidity. Gone were those creepy childish assumptions, replaced with the boring thought of how hot and muggy this would make an area already hot and humid even worse.

Back to Cliff. Once again, Roger thought, *'Now, where did he go?'*

Roger walked over to the far side of the grove and saw another footprint. As he glanced up along what appeared to be an old trail, Roger saw another stand of trees, but this one seemed even more significant and denser.

Roger thought, *'I'll bet he ran over there to take shelter after a few loud booms of thunder hit us. I know I would have done the same thing.'*

Roger took off following the old path. Halfway to the next stand of trees, he saw another footprint that looked a lot like the ones he'd seen in the other area. Roger was sure this had to have been made by Cliff.

As Roger got to the next tree stand, he ducked into the area and noted how much darker it was here than it had been in the previous location. Roger assumed Cliff had to have figured getting over to this stand with its denser tree canopy would be safer than the one he had been huddled in.

Roger shook his head and thought, '*Smart boy.*'

Just as Roger ducked into the stand of trees and his eyes adjusted to the dimmer light, he saw what appeared to be a sizeable military camouflage-type net lying on the ground. As he continued looking around the area, he determined that a rope had been attached to a pulley system on one of the other trees. There was no rope, but the netting on the ground looked recently disturbed. Roger was no wartime buff, but he knew enough to understand that this looked like a booby trap, not just some random net that someone may have left here on a previous hunting trip.

As he continued to survey the area, Roger thought again, '*Now, why in the world would anyone want to booby trap their land? Unless they are doing something, they don't want others to discover. Something illegal?*'

Roger was instantly alarmed. As he continued to look around the area and glanced back in the direction he had come, he noticed the downed fence and the fence post that was running perpendicular to their property line and realized that he and Cliff must have passed over their property line.

Most of the fencing was down, and there was much underbrush, so Roger could see how Cliff easily missed this and ran across the neighboring property. From experience,

Roger knew that when running for cover in the middle of a storm, you're not always looking as closely at your surroundings as you usually should be.

Usually, this wasn't a huge issue. Most of the time, a land surveyor could quickly apologize and back off an adjoining property. But we were in rural Florida, and there were many crazy people out there these days who took property ownership very seriously.

Roger kicked himself for having broken his radio. He couldn't radio Cliff to check to see that he was okay, and he couldn't radio back to home base to advise Tom and Brent that something had happened. Roger decided he would have to continue West to see if he could find Cliff.

'*This is not what I need on my plate today,*' Roger thought. As he surveyed the clearing under the trees, he chanted, "Not only does Cliff not follow instructions, but he makes rash decisions, and then one of us has to pick up the slack."

Roger continued heading west and exited the tree stand. He looked down and saw a spot where there were several footprints, not just one set. Based on the number of prints, two other individuals had joined Cliff. This wasn't looking good. Roger was getting worried. He continued west along this old trail. He was cautious and made a concerted effort not to step on twigs or kick rocks or dirt. Of course, this made his trek that much slower, but in Roger's mind, it's better to be slow, methodical, and quiet, especially when you're potentially stalking someone.

Roger noticed a little camp area as he crested the next small hill. He hunkered down in the underbrush so he wouldn't be as noticeable on top of this hill. He slowly edged himself closer to the area. As he got closer, he could better understand who was at this camp and what was happening. Roger remembered he had packed his binoculars when they headed out this morning. He is an amateur wildlife enthusiast, so he wanted to have them in case he saw something notable worth viewing.

As Roger brought the binoculars to his eyes, he was shocked while looking toward this little camp area. Tanks, tubes, glass jars, firewood, and other devices and attachments were placed in some ordered assembly. He continued looking at this setup and realized this was an illegal moonshine still. When he was younger, he had read about these in history books and was fascinated by the entire illegal booze-running era during Prohibition. So, he knew a moonshine still when he saw one.

'*OH, BOY,*' thought Roger, '*This is all we need.*'

Roger had often heard that moonshiners are a tough breed of people, and if they are ever infringed upon, they shoot first and then ask questions. The hairs on the back of

Roger's neck stood up in nervous attention, and he proceeded to move off the path but toward the moonshine still area. He had to ensure that what he was viewing was actually what he thought it was.

As Roger inched closer to the campsite, he hunkered down again and lifted the binoculars to his eyes. Roger saw something, immediately pulled the binoculars away from his face, shook his head, wiped his eyes, and then looked through the lenses again. He was shocked at what he saw.

Roger saw two thick-muscled men mauling one another's mouths while groping each other's bodies. In front of them, while they kneeled, was Cliff, and he was tied up and hanging from a tree. The weirdest part was that it appeared Cliff was eagerly participating with them. He saw that the two men had pulled Cliff toward them while they kneeled. Cliff's bulging crotch was at eye level with his captors. They would break their kissing, swoop in, lick, spit on, and mouth Cliff's bulge, and then return to kissing.

Roger saw Cliff's head fall back each time one of the men put their hot mouths over his rock-hard bulge. Roger noted that the mound in Cliff's shorts was getting wetter and wetter with every lick and kiss he received.

Roger was shocked and thought, '*How could his workmate, Cliff, not share with him that he was gay? Wait, Cliff, gay? No friggin way.*' He glanced through the binoculars again. The two muscled guys Roger saw at the campsite had now grabbed Cliff's crotch. Cliff moaned loudly.

Roger was close enough to hear Cliff moaning as the brothers continued swabbing his bulge with their hot, juicy mouths. He suddenly saw the larger guy of the two on their knees, stand up, and quickly remove what appeared to be a sweaty, dirty old jockstrap. When he pulled the jock down his hips, as it passed over his throbbing cock, the guy's cock leaped to attention, smacking his rigid lower abs and bouncing up and down, almost like a "sprung" spring. As the other man stayed on his knees, wetting Cliff's crotch, the bigger man took his dirty jockstrap and quickly rammed it into Cliff's open moaning mouth. It looked like Cliff initially tried to spit the cloth out of his mouth. He shook his head from left to right.

As Roger secretly watched from afar, the guy with the jock seemed pleased to see his sweaty smelly jock rammed into his captive's mouth. He quickly grabbed a roll of duct tape off a table near the still and wrapped a couple of layers over Cliff's mouth. Roger could tell that this had quieted any audible moans coming from Cliff. As the big man finished with the duct tape, Roger could see the man's huge cock bouncing every time he moved. His erection was thick and had a slight downward curve, finished with an ample amount of foreskin that drooped over the head of his cock. Marcus's cock bounced at a ninety-degree angle from his groin, and with every bounce, you could see his thick furry pubes wafting in the breeze.

While Marcus finished securing Cliff's mouth, his throbbing cock bounced and suddenly slapped his brother's cheek. Instantly, a long, clear, sticky string of precum smeared all over Pete's stubbled face. Pete leaned over and grabbed Marcus's cock. Marcus jumped for a second, but suddenly, in his sex-crazed state, he thrust his hips forward, and Pete stuck his tongue out and began licking Marcus's dripping cock.

Marcus continued thrusting his hips forward and back, and each forward movement would cause his hard, sticky cock to press against his brother's mouth. Marcus flicked and twisted Cliff's nipples. Cliff wiggled and shook but appeared to be enjoying this attention.

Again, Roger scratched his head and thought, '*I would have never known.*' But as he continued watching, he wondered if Cliff was into this or going along because tied as he was, he obviously couldn't get away. Roger thought it strange that Cliff would be all tied up and do all of this while on the clock at work if it was of his choosing. Cliff may be young and didn't always rationally think things through, but Roger knew Cliff was reliable enough that he would never do something like this while working. Roger surmised Cliff was going along with all of this to keep from being brutalized by the moonshiners.

At this point, Roger realized that with Cliff captured and tied up, there was no way he'd be able to get Cliff's radio to radio for help from the survey base camp. He would have to return to the survey base camp and alert Tom and Cliff about what had happened. He hated leaving Cliff at the mercy of his two captives but felt he had no choice but to go for help. Considering the size and stature of the two men holding Cliff, Roger vowed he needed backup and would not try and fight these two muscle bears alone to free Cliff.

Roger mentally calculated that he could return to their campsite within an hour if he moved quickly. He glanced at his watch and noted it was already after 4:00. He and Cliff were expected back at camp by 6:00. If they didn't show, he was confident Tom, Brent, or both would go hunting for them. He also surmised that if he took off now, he could get to camp before 6:00 and warn his superiors of what was transpiring here, and they could reach the authorities to save Cliff, and it would be best to get back to him before darkness fell, which could make a rescue effort fruitless.

Roger hunkered down a bit more, checked his surroundings, backed away from the moonshine still, turned, and began running east, through both forested areas, across the neighboring fence line, and heading to base camp. He only hoped he could get to Tom and Brent, and they could return before anything terrible happened. Roger's nervous gate quickly turned into a jog. He was careful not to move too quickly because he didn't want to accidentally slam into a branch, trip, fall, and harm himself. He needed to get back to camp and warn his teammates.

Chapter Thirteen

As Roger returned to the survey crew's base camp, he could hear what sounded like an orchestra of really off-key and sharply squeaking electric guitar strings whining. He'd never heard anything like it. It wasn't unpleasant, but the odd screeches did have an unsettling effect. He was shocked that the sound he was hearing would come and go, almost as if he had heard something, but he wasn't sure if he had heard something. He glanced back and saw what looked like a swarm of strange insects. He continued jogging and often looked back to see a few insects still following.

As the sun occasionally popped out of the clouds, Roger noticed this swarming mass would take on a shiny greenish glow as the sun reflected off the insects' body structure. The swarm seemed to undulate, increasing and decreasing in size and shape. Imagine many birds flying in unison in the sky and their wings causing their flight to waft, twist, and curl.

As Roger looked back again, he hadn't noticed a hole left by a fallen tree and tripped. Roger gasped as he fell to the ground. He was breathing heavily from jogging and slowly started to push himself off of the earth. As he attempted to get back to his feet, he heard that strange sound and saw the swarm hover over him and then rapidly move away, heading east. A few stragglers lingered behind and hovered, zipping and zapping, on the slight breeze. Roger looked at this strange bug better as he watched the mosquitoes as they raced away from him, heading toward the survey team's camp.

He noted the size and coloring differences of the weird mosquitoes, noting they appeared to be some mutant form of the standard and annoying blood-sucker.

'I sure hope the guys at camp see those things coming because I've never seen mosquitoes act like that,' he thought as he started jogging again. As he continued toward their work camp, he noted that none of the mosquitoes were interested in him. Although a few stragglers had hung behind the swarm, they seemed to hover for a few minutes and then took off following the rest of their "herd."

Roger remembered that he usually wasn't terribly bothered by mosquitoes, and on a few camping trips, his friends had pointed fingers and jealously accused him of performing some special magic which would explain why everyone else on that trip came home like one giant itchy bite, and he returned home unblemished.

As Roger attempted to return to the survey team's camp, Pete and Marcus continued their aggressive, manly onslaught of kissing, rubbing, caressing, and manhandling. The brothers would grab one another's throbbing nipples and yank. It seemed like they were playing some competitive game to see who could yank the other's nipples harder and get the best reaction. All the while, they were licking, kissing, and spitting into one another's mouths.

Marcus quickly shoved his fingers into the waistband of his brother's underwear and yanked them down. Pete's throbbing 8" cock suddenly bounced out in the open. As Pete looked down at his bouncing cock, Marcus grabbed it and yanked. Pete's head fell back, his mouth opened, his eyes closed, and he moaned sensually.

Pete returned the favor, reached down, and grabbed Marcus's throbbing cock. As the brother's hands reached one another's cocks, they stood kissing. Cliff could see their mouths working, tongues lashing and fighting, and saliva dripping.

Marcus and Pete were thrashing one another's dicks with their hands. At one point, they both stopped, squeezing each other's dicks at the base and shaking them. With thick furry pubes falling over their hands as they banged against each other's rock-hard guts, they continued stroking and caressing their throbbing cocks.

The brothers pulled back, leered at one another, stroked each other's cocks hard, let out deep evil groans, and laughed. As they began kissing again, they rubbed each other and, with their other hands, pulled Cliff toward them again. Cliff was helpless in his bindings. They continued pulling on him and pulled him closer to them, yet again.

As the brothers stood before Cliff, his wet crotch rubbed against their hairy thighs. Cliff gasped as he felt his throbbing cock, still covered by his shorts, pulled against both of his captor's bodies, causing his hard cock to bang against their thighs. There was something sensual about feeling his cock, and balls slammed against these two hot and brawny men before him.

Marcus took his hand off Pete's hard cock, reached toward Cliff, placed his warm hand over Cliff's crotch, grasped Cliff's zipper, and pulled down so hard that the zipper broke and ripped out of the bottom of his work shorts. As the crotch of Cliff's shorts ripped open, his hard-on was snaking its way through his boxer briefs, and his dick stood out, pressing his underwear through the broken fly of his shorts and pointing toward Pete and Marcus's bouncing cocks.

Pete and Marcus turned and looked at Cliff. They tightened their grip on Cliff's ass cheeks, pulled him closer, and suddenly Pete and Marcus began licking, nuzzling, and kissing Cliff's face and neck. Cliff didn't understand what was going on but was aware that each time one of the brothers touched him, it felt like a molten hot poker had pierced his skin all over his body.

The brothers released their grip on their cocks, quickly reached over, and grabbed Cliff's throbbing, underwear-covered cock. As they both grabbed his cock, Cliff uncontrollably arched his back and pushed his body closer to them.

Cliff's underwear was sticky and wet with the precum he had begun ejaculating from the drugs and venom coursing through his veins. Marcus and Pete continued to mutually stroke Cliff's throbbing cock. You could hear the slopping sounds as they rubbed Cliff's precum into his underwear.

Cliff found it hard to concentrate, and gone were any thoughts that what was happening here was wrong. All he knew was that he couldn't get enough of these men touching and caressing him. As this continued, Marcus and Pete looked deeply into Cliff's eyes and began removing the duct tape and jock strap. As they reached to remove Marcus's sweaty, sticky jock strap from Cliff's mouth, Cliff sucked the jock as they pulled it from his mouth. He savored the mix of his saliva, Marcus's precum, and sweat from the jock. The three men could smell the bittersweet scent of Marcus's sweaty, sticky jock on Cliff's breath as he breathed out.

As Marcus removed the jockstrap, Pete and Cliff leaned toward one another. Pete's thick, rough tongue suddenly invaded Cliff's sweaty, juicy mouth. Cliff leaned against the rope confines as he and Pete kissed.

Pete and Marcus continued stroking Cliff's throbbing cock through his shorts. Marcus watched his older brother making out with this hot young guy and quickly moved his head closer, and, in a flash, lips, tongues, and mouths were smashed together as all three men began raping one another's mouths.

Cliff's body sizzled. The feeling of his captors' tongues raping his mouth felt so wild. He had never kissed another man, so he had no idea that a man's tongue felt rougher than any woman's tongue he'd ever sucked on. The men's tongues on Cliff felt like sandpaper, and every scruffy lick sent waves of pleasure through his body. He felt Pete and Marcus refocus and start sucking on his ever-hardening nipples. He'd never had sensitive nipples before, but for some reason, his nipples were hyper-sensitive. Feeling two rough scruffy men's faces rubbing his face while their tongues continually assaulted his mouth, Cliff rocked his body back and forth, pushing his throbbing cock in and out of the brothers' grip. Cliff thrust his dick back and forth as the brothers held it tightly, still sheathed in his boxer briefs.

Marcus stopped kissing and took his hand off Cliff's dick. Cliff looked at Marcus, arched his back again, thrust his cock into Pete's fist, and yearned to feel Marcus back on his body, but Marcus had other ideas.

Marcus quickly picked up his hunting knife and held it to Cliff's shirt. Cliff looked Marcus in the eyes, fearing maybe this wouldn't end well. Marcus took the knife, leaned in, kissed Cliff and Pete, and started gently but forcefully slashing at Cliff's shirt. As he continued cutting the fabric of Cliff's shirt, he pulled away the tattered pieces, but it became apparent that the ropes holding Cliff were strategically placed. As soon as his shirt was gone, he felt the ropes binding his chest slowly begin rubbing his erect and throbbing nipples. The rough twine of the ropes excited Cliff. He was drooling as he and the brothers continued to kiss.

The brothers would roll the ropes near Cliff's nipples up and down. This caused the rough twine to roll up in one direction, over the top of Cliff's hardening nipples, and then they would roll it down, and it would pass over Cliff's nipples yet again. Each time the rope assaulted Cliff's nipples, he saw stars and heard missiles shooting inside his head.

Cliff found himself uncontrollably writhing to meet each roll of the rope with his nipples to receive the maximum burning and pinching effect. Cliff was turning into a nipple whore.

As Marcus and Pete rolled the rope back and forth, between each roll, one or the other brother would reach up, grab one of Cliff's hard nipples, and twist, causing Cliff to moan, groan, and hunch his body from the pain and excitement of being molested.

Marcus moved lower on Cliff's body and quickly cut and ripped through Cliff's shorts and underwear. The ropes kept the cut clothing from falling away from Cliff's body. Pete and Cliff continued their tongue battle, and Marcus and Pete began tugging and pulling out the tatters of Cliff's shorts.

Pete sat down and admired the stiff bulge from Cliff's tattered shorts. He grabbed the waistband of Cliff's underwear and yanked downward with full force. Cliff could hear the fabric of his shorts ripping. The tension of the ripping material pulling against Cliff's groin was hot yet almost unbearable. Cliff, once again, bucked and bucked from the pleasure and pain.

Once all of the pieces of Cliff's clothing had been pulled away, he hung helplessly as the brothers continued to grope and caress his hard body. Cliff couldn't understand why he was so turned onto all of this, but again, his brain was compromised by the drugs and venom. Even though he'd have a fleeting thought that what he was doing was not "normal," that thought would quickly disappear, only to be replaced with a more intensely hot feeling that he must be molested and owned by these hot, sexy men.

Marcus placed his mouth back on Cliff's again. Pete pulled away, walked over to the moonshine still, and came back with a small wad of twine. Marcus and Cliff continued kissing. Marcus pinched and twisted Cliff's nipples, and

Cliff eagerly moved his body to receive as much contact from the manly swamp guy as possible.

As the fabric of Cliff's underwear gave way, Pete looked Cliff in the eye until Cliff stopped bucking. Cliff was breathing heavily and glaring back at Pete. Pete grabbed Cliff's cock and balls and twisted them, and began tightly wrapping the twine around them.

As Cliff's mouth was still being assaulted, the expression on his face changed from pain to pleasure and pain. After a few minutes, Cliff pulled away from Marcus's kisses and looked down. He saw that his dick and balls had been wrapped tightly. The blood in his hard cock was held there, and his cock continued to engorge more. Cliff's cock looked like a giant hard, bouncing baseball bat.

Cliff was now hanging fully nude and helpless. His hands and arms were tied behind him. His ankles were bound and pulled up toward his ass. He was freely swinging out in the middle of these swampy woods. The thought of being held helpless and being ruggedly handled by two hot, swarthy, hairy men made Cliff's body quake and shiver.

Pete stood up and returned his focus to Cliff's mouth. Pete and Marcus placed their calloused hands back on Cliff's hard cock. The brothers began kissing Cliff again. Marcus moved down to Cliff's nipples and licked and slurped on them while Pete continued stroking Cliff's cock and raping Cliff's mouth.

With the "Kweer Skeeter" venom raging through their veins, Pete dropped to his knees again. In the bat of an eye, Pete was now face to face with his brother's throbbing cock and the hot dripping cock of his captive. Pete quickly licked the head of Marcus's cock. After one lick, he moved over and licked Cliff's cock. Cliff and Marcus mouthed one another and moaned.

Pete looked up at the two men kissing, dived toward Cliff's dick, and swallowed the entire cock, all the way to Cliff's bushy pubes. Cliff had never felt something like this. No girl he had ever been with was capable or wanted to suck him as deeply as Pete was now sucking him.

Cliff rocked his hips back and forth. His tongue felt raw from sucking and being sucked on by Marcus's rough, scratchy tongue. Cliff could smell Pete and Marcus's manly, sweaty musk as the three men continued grinding on one another.

Pete deepthroated Cliff's dick. Pete grabbed Cliff's ass cheeks and pulled Cliff's dick as deep as he could. At the same time, Marcus pulled his mouth off Cliff's, grabbed the back of Cliff's head, lifted his muscular hairy arm to expose his wet, musky armpit, and forcefully pushed Cliff's face into his thick, damp pit. Cliff was shocked at suddenly feeling like he might suffocate as his entire face was buried into Marcus's wet, raunchy pit, and the only breath he could get would be a wet, sweat-infused one. But as if on auto-pilot, he suddenly started licking and nibbling at the base of Marcus's pit hair. The bittersweet taste of sweat and musk had Cliff rocking his body. Tilting his body made Cliff's dick go deeper into Pete's mouth. The three men were going at it like high school teenagers. No body part was left untouched as the brothers continued their sexual onslaught.

As Pete continued swallowing Cliff's throbbing, dripping cock, Marcus moved away. Again, Cliff felt a sense of loss as neither Marcus's hands nor mouth touched him. His panic quickly gave way to lust when he felt the heat of Marcus's body suddenly standing behind him as he continued to swing in his roped cocoon.

Marcus roughly pressed his body into Cliff's backside. Marcus dropped a thick load of spit on his stiff cock. He then spit in his hand and rubbed deep into Cliff's hairy ass crack. Cliff, again, had a panicked thought that this was not right. Men don't do this to one another. As he felt something thick and hard pressing against his asshole, he felt the cool breeze waft into his ass crack. He realized, again, that Marcus had pulled his ass cheeks apart, exposing his pink cherry rosebud. The cooler air on Cliff's hole made him shiver as both brothers held him.

Pete was rhythmically going up and down on Cliff's cock while caressing Cliff's hairy muscled thighs. Marcus was slowly pushing his dick at Cliff's hole. Cliff tensed, but Marcus wrapped his arms around him and flicked his nipples. Cliff was in heaven. He had never had this much attention performed on his body all at the same time. As Cliff continued to feel his hole slowly opening and closing around Marcus's dick, he felt wave after wave of hot pleasure course through his body. He found himself pushing back, ever so slightly, against the hard thing pressing at his asshole.

Then, Marcus presented another little "thing" he had gotten from the chick he had recently pounded. It was a little brown bottle, about the size of an eye-drop bottle. Marcus stood behind Cliff. Cliff's back was arched. Cliff could feel the head of Marcus's dick pushing and pushing. Stealthily, Marcus shook the brown bottle. When he cracked the lid, a sharp hiss occurred. Marcus had discovered poppers.

As Pete held Cliff's body still and Marcus stood behind Cliff, he leaned over and wrapped his arms around Cliff, bringing the brown bottle to his left nostril. Cliff didn't know what to do and began to panic. Marcus held Cliff's head and forced the bottle under his nose, saying, "Inhale." Cliff tried to shake his head, but to no avail. He finally breathed some of the fumes from the bottle and instantly stopped struggling. Marcus held the bottle to Cliff's right nostril and said, "Inhale." This time around, Cliff took an intense breath.

With his mouth, Pete quickly engulfed Cliff's dick again, swallowed, and sucked hard. At the same time, the poppers Cliff had inhaled caused his tight virgin hole to relax, almost as if it had been numbed. The head of Marcus's dick made a "popping" sound as it finally broke the entrance to Cliff's virgin hole. Cliff saw stars and felt unbelievable pain. As he snapped out of his trance, he suddenly tried to pull away from Marcus because the pain was so intense, and all he thought about was to get that hard throbbing thing out of his tight virgin hole. Marcus, anticipating Cliff's reaction, grabbed Cliff's hips, pulled him tighter, and buried his cock deep. Cliff had never known such pleasure, and as he was involuntarily pushing himself to get fucked by another man, his head was reeling with the pleasure he felt from Pete's rough scruffy face and tongue sucking him to the base of his dick each time.

The poppers did nothing but take every sensation Cliff experienced and exacerbate it ten-fold. He hung in his roped confines and felt Pete's scruffy face, beard, and mustache raking over his dick, back and forth, saliva dripping, a white foam forming along Cliff's dick as Pete's sucking increased in speed. Cliff's dick was on fire. He was thrusting his hips as much as he could while restrained.

The pain in Cliff's ass had subsided a little because he could thrust and swing away from Marcus ever so slightly. Again, this pushed his dick deeper down Pete's throat, keeping Marcus's massive cock from ripping into his ass. Or so Cliff thought. Just when he thought he had avoided further pain from Marcus, Cliff realized he had buried his cock to the bush in Pete's mouth, and he could go no further. Again, Cliff felt that hard, yet fleshy, head of Marcus's cock pushing at his back door.

Cliff tried one more time to pull away, but he was held too tightly by Pete's mouth and Marcus's hands holding his body. The sound of that popping occurred again. Cliff arched his back, and suddenly, Marcus started ramming his spit-covered dick into Cliff's hairy asshole. Cliff's eyes flew open, and he moaned.

Pete could taste precum leaking out of Cliff's hard cock as his brother's dick began to invade Cliff's virgin hole. Tasting this young buck's hot precum caused Pete's infected brain to go into overdrive, and he began thrusting his head on and off Cliff's dick. He'd pull off Cliff's dick and slap the stiff throbbing shaft against Cliff's rigid abs. He'd then beat his mouth and face with Cliff's hard cock, leaving trails of precum all over his scruffy cheeks and chin.

Suddenly, Marcus was buried deeply inside Cliff. Cliff's body stiffened as he realized the massive younger guy's dick had entirely impaled him. The pain was almost unbearable. Pete could feel Cliff's dick throbbing as his asshole massaged and caressed every inch of Marcus's cock as it slowly slid in and out of his ass. Cliff didn't think he could continue this but had no way of stopping it. Then Marcus's thick cock found Cliff's man pussy, deep inside his ass.

Again, Cliff wasn't even aware there was such a thing on his body, and when Marcus found that spot, Cliff felt such waves of pleasure that he felt his body lifted off of this planet and shot into the far reaches of the universe. The sense of euphoria was incredible. Cliff had never experienced something so intense.

As Cliff's tight wet hole finally began to accommodate Marcus's massive cock, Cliff started to feel the severe pain from earlier subside, and a new feeling took prevalence. Cliff started feeling a hot and steamy burning sensation inside his gut. He started feeling hot flashes coursing through his body. He would ram his cock down his captor's throat, and upon pulling his hips away from that hot mouth, he'd find himself burying his tight ass on his other captor's hard cock. Cliff was fucking himself on Marcus's cock while fucking Pete's mouth.

As Cliff's body slowly succumbed to the pleaser Pete and Marcus inflicted upon him, he picked up the pace. His body began to involuntarily push deeply onto Marcus's cock and then into Pete's mouth. Cliff's rhythm picked up in speed and intensity. His hips were now a blur as he was fucked by Marcus and fucking Pete's mouth.

Pete suddenly jumped up, kissed Cliff and Marcus wetly, and turned around. Marcus stared at Pete and was surprised when he saw Pete spit into his hand and reach around to insert that into his hole. Marcus had always looked up to Pete as the older brother and the tough guy but was surprised and turned on by the fact that his brother seemed to be acting more passive than he thought possible.

As Pete broke off his kisses, he spit again and rubbed this all over Cliff's cock. Cliff was moaning and sucking breath into his mouth as his ass was being assaulted by Marcus's cock. Pete turned his back to Cliff and backed against him. Cliff was ecstatic and surprised when he felt Pete grab his stiff cock and slowly start sliding it into his ass. Once Pete got Cliff's dick to penetrate his asshole, he quickly and assuredly pushed onto Cliff's dick. Cliff gasped, moaned, and slumped back against Marcus. Now Marcus was buried deep inside Cliff's ass, and Cliff was buried deep inside Pete's ass.

The three horned-up men subconsciously adjusted their rhythm, and within a few seconds, all three were humping in unison. Cliff would thrust back against Marcus's cock as it penetrated him deeply, only to have Marcus's thrusting push Cliff's dick deeper and deeper into Pete's ass.

Cliff was suspended from the tree in his roped cocoon and bounced like a pendulum between one man's dick invading his ass and his dick invading the other man's ass.

Marcus thrust and thrust his cock into Cliff's hole. Cliff felt his dick burning and throbbing as it was forced into Pete's asshole. Cliff could feel Pete's ass muscles hugging and grasping at his cock, almost causing Cliff's cock to stretch as he pulled out because Pete's ass was like a vacuum and kept sucking and holding Cliff's cock inside his ass.

Sweat was forming on the three men. The campsite was quiet, save for a slight breeze, and three men groaning, moaning, and panting in the afternoon heat. Sweat was running down Marcus's legs. You could see the hair on Cliff's thighs getting wet and sticky with Marcus's sweat.

Sweat was dripping off Cliff's chest and landing all over Pete's hairy back and ass. The men continued fucking powerfully. Slapping, slurping, and wet body contact sounds emanating from the campsite as the three men devoured one another.

Without much warning, Cliff started getting that familiar feeling that he would shoot his load. He quickened the pace at which he was fucking Pete. As Cliff's pumping increased speed, Marcus noted that Cliff's ass began to aggressively milk his throbbing cock. This caused Marcus to increase his thrusting speed.

As if on cue, Cliff's thick cock jerked intensely inside Pete's ass, and he began spewing his manly load deep inside Pete's hairy hole. Cliff had never had an orgasm like this. He could feel his entire body curling from the effects of this earth-shattering moment when he exploded. Marcus's mouth was near Cliff's ear just as this intense feeling sent Cliff into overdrive. He could feel Marcus's hot breath on his ear as Marcus whimpered and whispered, "I'm gonna bury your hole on my dick, stud."

As Cliff was slowing his pace inside Pete's ass and relishing the feeling of Pete's muscles milking his ejaculating cock, he felt Marcus's cock swell to the point where it felt his ass muscles would pop like a balloon. The fullness was so intense that it made Cliff suddenly stop moving. Marcus's ragged breath and scruffy face brushed against Cliff's ear, and Marcus said, "All for you, you fucking hot fuck!" And like that, Cliff felt gush after gush of thick hot wet cum filling his insides. Marcus licked and nibbled Cliff's ear and said, "Yeah, that's the way to fuck."

Cliff could feel Marcus's hard cock deep inside his hole. Marcus made no attempts to pull out. As Cliff remained swinging in his roped confines, with Marcus's dick still throbbing inside his ass, he could feel his cum slowly leaking out of Pete's ass and see it trickling down his furry legs. Neither of the three men seemed willing or able to pull off the other. All three hung there, slowly caressing, pushing in and out, and rocking.

Pete quickly started stroking his hard cock. The feeling of Cliff's still hard cock deep inside his asshole was driving him crazy. He had never felt so tight and full before. Pete was all about fucking tight pussies. He'd never even considered doing anything with a man. After all, that's not natural. Right?

Those thoughts were somewhat fleeting, as Pete could feel Cliff's hard body heaving as he slowly came down from his orgasm. Just as Cliff and Marcus stopped rocking their bodies, Pete's dick exploded. He stroked, thick jets of cum blasted all over his abs and then down onto his hairy thighs. He quickly grabbed some of the fresh hot sticky cum and licked his fingers. He thought, '*What the F?*' But then he reached for more hot cum and licked his fingers again.

As Cliff leaned back against Marcus, Pete leaned back against Cliff. They leaned so their mouths were close enough to kiss or lick from behind. Cliff could taste the sweet and salty cum from Pete's mouth as they kissed. Sweat was dripping all over the ground, but the three men seemed lost in a trance and continued to hold, caress, and grind one another while their tongues licked and wrestled.

No one realized that in addition to the crazy effects of the "KWEER Skeeter" bites inflicted on these men, taking an infected man's load in one's mouth or ass would prolong the gay effects of the bite. In other words, the mosquito bite would initiate the libido conversion, but if men took loads in their mouths or asses by those infected, those loads included ingredients that would prolong the gay effect. If men continued having sex and ejaculating and the cum was ingested, the gay libido effect continued and would slowly but surely dissipate, but this would take quite a bit of time and require there be no further contact with the "KWEER Skeeters."

As Marcus, Pete, and Cliff slowly came down from their sexual high, just a few yards away, if you listened closely, you could now hear that new, yet familiar, screeching and squeaking sound. Those "Kweer Skeeters" were still out there buzzing around.

Chapter Fourteen

Roger was trying to get back to camp so he could warn Tom and Brent and they could get back to the moonshine still to save Cliff. All Roger could think was how quickly things had gone from a typical job issue to an emergency crisis, and he was trying not to panic but to keep a level head and get help.

At the survey camp, the storm had finally passed. Brent and I had taken cover in the office tent. Either tent would have worked fine, but we felt it better to be near our equipment just in case we needed to sacrifice ourselves and throw ourselves over it.

The lightning and thunder were pretty intense. There was rain and a few wind gusts, but the storm passed quickly. I sure hoped the boys hadn't gotten slammed by this passing storm.

As the clouds started to part and bits of sunlight began to pop in and out, Brent and I stepped out of the tent to take inventory of our surroundings. Everything seemed okay. A couple of little items had blown across the clearing, but for the most part, everything was still intact.

As Brent and I picked up the few scattered items, I glanced to the West. The clouds were breaking up a little, but as I looked, it appeared like a bank of black clouds was moving lower on the horizon. At first, I was afraid this was another storm, but suddenly, I heard a high-pitched, unearthly screeching sound. It was unusual because if I turned my head, I could hear something faint, but as soon as I moved, the sound would quickly stop, only to return as I moved my head to another position.

I caught myself sticking an index finger in each of my ears and giving them that little yank like you've got an itch you can't seem to get deep inside your ear. The sound didn't go away, and just about the time I was convinced I had developed ringing of the ears, we saw a swarm of something heading our way.

Brent approached me as we placed the last few items near the tent. He said, "What the heck is that?" and pointed to the sky. I nodded and told him I had also seen this.

As we continued to stare at the strange formation in the sky, Brent suddenly shouted, "Hey, that's no storm; those are bugs." He yelled, "Damn, those are some strange-looking mosquitoes." As he finished his comment, they were upon us. That screaming sound was much louder now. We could make out the individual insects as they swarmed toward our camp, their bodies shimmering and reflecting the sunlight like little green flashes of light.

As Brent and I stood transfixed by the sight of the swarming "skeeters," Brent took off running toward the tent area of our camp. I didn't move quickly enough, and I was attacked by not one, not two, but multiple mosquitoes. Each sting or bite was excruciatingly painful. But as soon as the pain began, it rapidly subsided, and a warm sense of euphoria overwhelmed me. I can't explain, but it felt like floating on a warm sea. My entire body tingled, almost to the point of feeling ticklish. I gave out a low, involuntary growl. That euphoria caressed my body and mind to a level of intensity that caused me to close my eyes tightly and rub them. My ears were ringing, and my body felt suddenly chilled, but almost as soon as the chill occurred, it disappeared, only to be replaced with another burning sensation in my groin. I snapped out of whatever trance I had fallen into, only long enough to realize that I felt so horny that I could only think about getting my dick out of the confines of my shorts and getting off. I would have gladly fucked any knothole in any tree. It felt like I was a teenager again and unable to control my libido or my ever-swollen cock.

As this new horny slutty feeling washed over me, I let out another involuntary moan followed by a chuckle as I suddenly thought, '*Poor Mom, if only she knew what a nasty filthy-minded slut of a son she had raised.*' I laughed out loud at this as I remembered the only time my mother ever caught me doing "the nasty," I happened to be off work on a random Saturday. I was 19 at the time and still living with the folks. Mom had gone shopping, which usually meant she'd be gone for several hours. Dad was helping one of his friends work on the large property he had acquired. They were tearing down some old outbuildings or something.

I drove into the neighboring town, stopped at the X-rated porn shop, grabbed a couple of fuck magazines, and ran home to enjoy a little "me" time before family stuff got in the way again.

It was a warm spring day. The windows in the house were open. A gentle breeze was wafting in and out. I was in my room with the door closed, lying on my bed, naked, surrounded by the new mags I had purchased, just stroking my huge dick, and, "BOOM," suddenly the bedroom door swings open, and there's Mom in her Saturday shopping attire, staring at me with her hand still on the doorknob.

She stared at me. I stared at her. I held my dick in my hand. She said, "Oh, I'm sorry. I thought the wind blew the door shut, and I didn't think you were home." She broke eye contact with me, dipped her head, slowly backed out of the room, and shut my bedroom door.

Needless to say, I don't think I finished the "chore" I set out to do that day. I stayed in my room for what I considered the appropriate time to pass and did my business as usual. Nothing was ever repeated.

I have often wondered how she could say she didn't think I was home when she had to pass by my parked vehicle in the driveway when she pulled into the garage. Maybe a little ironically strange?

Anyway, back to my current predicament…

My crotch burned and felt hot, like the blast of heat from a well-prepared BBQ grill when you popped open the cover to check the meat. The way it felt, I hoped and prayed my flesh wouldn't be cooked well done. My dick started swelling. Thoughts kept racing through my mind, '*What the fuck is happening? I'm not like this. I'm in control. I don't allow anything to control me.*'

I started jumping around as the searing pain from the bites I had received continued coursing through my body. I kept feeling wave after wave of hot flashes. I would rub and pat the back of my neck where the mosquito bites had occurred. The waves of pain were like electric sparks. They would start in my balls, cause my dick to jump to attention, then thrust up through my abdomen, ignite my hard nipples and make them throb, shoot to my mouth where I began to produce a large amount of saliva, and then back down to my groin where the searing heat would slam into my scrotum like a nuclear fission reaction.

As I hopped around like a madman, jerking and flexing my over-stimulated body, I was unaware that Brent had run to the sleeping tent and barricaded himself there. I kept feeling waves of uncontrollable horniness flow through my body. I would have hot flashes; then my dick would suddenly push against my shorts, and my asshole would begin twitching, almost like it was having spasms. I caught myself running my fingers along my mouth, almost seductively. As much as I told myself this wasn't natural, all I could think about was getting my body naked and getting off. And I wanted a hot, sweaty, hard body to get off with. I yearned for physical contact with someone, anyone who was my masculine equal.

I shook my head and tried to think more clearly. My head felt foggy. As the burning sensation inside my body subsided, I looked around and noticed that Brent was gone. I yelled his name and heard nothing. The swarm was upon us so quickly that I hadn't seen him running or in what direction he ran.

I subconsciously rubbed the back of my neck as I looked around. I continued rubbing and caressing and then started running my hand down the open collar of my pullover shirt. I felt my thick, furry, sweaty chest hair spilling out over the collar at the neck. Immediately my dick tingled and started to swell some more. I ran my fingers through the fur. I pulled my hand back and felt the wetness from the sweat embedded under my chest hair as it coated my fingers; I sniffed my fingers, smelled the warm and bitter scent of my sweat, and without another thought, stuck my fingers into my mouth and sucked. I licked and sucked my fingers as if they were ice cream bars.

As I continued moving my fingers back from my chest to my mouth, I remembered Brent was with me before this happened. I looked around again and saw that the sleeping tent flap had been closed and secured. Brent must have run to that tent to avoid the swarming mosquitoes.

I thought, *'Smart man,'* and grabbed and tugged on my burning crotch.

I proceeded to walk toward the sleeping tent. As I moved toward the tent, my dick sprung to life inside my shorts. Sure, I've had erections my entire adult life. What average red-blooded man hasn't? But the timing of this erection was strange. I wasn't watching porn, I wasn't smoking pot, and I didn't see any sexy voluptuous naked women around. Yet, my cock was so hard that it felt like it was going to cut right through my underwear and my shorts, bursting through the fabric like the alien bursts through that guy's stomach in that crazy horror flick from years ago.

As I walked toward the tent, my balls banged back and forth against my legs, and that caused my throbbing cock to sway and bang back and forth inside my shorts and underwear. I grabbed my throbbing bulge to try and appease the raging monster making my dick so hard I couldn't walk normally. Touching my crotch, a large stream of drool spilled from my mouth and landed on my furry arm. I wiped my mouth with my hand and placed my hand on my chest over my right nipple. My nipples were growing harder and harder and starting to tingle almost painfully. Yet, each throb of my nipples would send more jets of fire to my groin, like the heat of a blow torch when used to fasten a rivet so pieces of metal can be bonded together permanently. I could feel the mosquito bites I'd received from that swarm. They were on the back of my neck, where I kept absentmindedly patting and caressing. I noticed two or three bites on my thighs as I assessed the bites on my neck. The skin felt puffy and itchy, but whenever I scratched near one of the infected areas, the hot flashes of fire that would shoot down my body and into my groin were so incredible that I caught myself audibly moaning.

I stopped and thought again, '*What the fuck is going on? Hell, I don't moan like this. I never moan like this when having hot, nasty sex.*' I scratched the itchy bites again, and another moan escaped my lips.

I caught myself absentmindedly rubbing my right nipple as it poked under the fabric of my shirt. I stopped walking, looked down, and noticed my shirt was wet right at the nipple. Some of the drool I had previously allowed drip from my mouth had dampened my shirt. The moist yet scratchy fabric rubbed against my nipple, sending more shockwaves to my dick and back.

My dick was pounding. My head was pounding. All I could think was that I had to get my dick off. If I didn't shoot a thick load of cum soon, I would explode, but not how I would typically like to explode.

I yelled for Brent. I started moving toward the tent again. I walked stiff-legged because every step would cause my dick to bend and roll in my shorts. I felt my balls twisting, my dick throbbing, and wet liquid spewing all over my underwear. I stopped, shook one of my legs, grabbed my crotch again, moaned, and took off toward the tent.

I yelled, "Brent, are you in there?"

Brent responded, "Yeah, damn, what the fuck was that?"

I stood hobbling on one leg and then the other. I thought, *'God damn, I want to cum so freaking badly.'* I looked down again and noticed a wet spot forming at the crotch of my shorts. The bulge in my shorts was so tight that it looked like the zipper at my crotch might rip open at any time.

I yelled at Brent and said, "Man, I think the swarm is gone. You can come out now." As I said this, I hopped from my right to my left leg and pushed down on the crotch of my shorts as my cock swelled more and more.

That thought again came to me: *'Damn, I want a hot body to touch, caress, and.... MOLEST.'*

Brent yelled from the tent, "Tom, are you OK? What are you doing out there? Did you get bitten by any of those bugs?"

I continued hopping and said, "Hey, I'm ok. I got bitten, and those stings hurt, but it was just a mosquito bite."

Brent answered back, "Oh, OK. Do you think it's safe to come back out? Has that swarm gone away?"

I wasn't sure why Brent was so cautious about little old mosquitoes, but Brent suddenly said, "I'm sorry I'm so cautious, but I have allergies and am allergic to some bug bites. I carry an EpiPen, but it doesn't work for mosquitoes, and their bite can still be more irritating for me than most."

For one lucid moment, I heard what Brent had said and understood, thinking, '*Gotcha, now I understand why you're being hesitant.*' However, right after that thought occurred, the fog returned to my brain, and the next idea I had was, '*I really need to touch your hot, sweaty body.*'

I grunted.

Brent yelled from inside the tent, "Did you say something?"

Although thoughts kept running through my head about wrestling Brent to the ground, or seeing him on his back with his legs in the air, or picturing me on top of him while he's tied to an old table, and my hips pounding him relentlessly, I just cleared my throat, trying to keep the tone of my voice calm and normal and said, "I just said it's ok to come out of the tent. The swarm is gone."

Again, my dick bobbed up and inside my shorts and underwear to the right. I hopped, grunted quietly, wrapped my hand around my crotch through my shorts, yanked on it, and punched it with my other hand. When Brent spoke, I began to notice how melodic his voice sounded. I noted how it had a deep, raspy tone. As Brent said, the vibrations of his voice sounded like music to my ears and also caused my dick to feel like it was vibrating like a worker bee in a giant hive. When he would speak, my dick performed summersaults in my pants.

I stopped hopping, and with my hand on my crotch, squeezing methodically, I thought, '*I'm not turned onto Brent's voice. Brent is a dude. He's my bro. I'm not gay. I love women.*'

As that thought rambled through my head, a louder voice started churning thoughts that began taking over my psyche. This new voice became louder and louder, drowning out all other ideas in my head. The deep, monotoned voice rang inside my head, saying, '*You must fuck hot wet holes. If you do not get it wet, your dick will dry up and drop off. Water will not do. Each time your dick throbs, it tells you to stop neglecting it.*'

That deep voice returned while my mind was engulfed in some self-prescribed and horny trance. The voice was the only thing I could now hear. The rest of my mind felt dark, empty, and at peace. The voice again said, '*Tom, you must strip off all of your clothing. Your body must feel human flesh close to it, tight to it, surrounded by it.*'

As the voice chanted inside my head, I could hear the sound of a zipper being pulled. Brent was slowly beginning to unzip the tent. I glanced at the tent and, through my foggy vision, saw the outer zipper core moving along the bottom of the opening.

My dick bounced so hard against my shorts that I feared it would bust my zipper. Without thinking twice, I reached down, grabbed my zipper flap, and pulled it down. The sound of the tent's door zipper slowly opening drowned out my unzipping and unbuttoning my shorts. My heartbeat was increasing, and it began to drown out the sound of both of the zippers.

As my shorts slowly fell low on my hips, I moved closer to the tent door. The anticipation of seeing Brent inside the tent made my body quiver like I was riding the rolling earth during a strong earthquake. I felt shaky, and I stood there wobbling just a little.

I looked down and noticed my nipples were still hard buttons, forcing protrusions to poke through the fabric of my shirt, and they were aching, also sending hot flashes to and from my groin. As if second nature, I reached for both nipples and twisted left and right, almost like dialing in some obscure news station on an old radio. As I continued turning my "knobs," more and more waves of pressure surged through my body, and my overzealous fingers were causing the fabric of my shirt to crease and wrinkle right at the spot where my nipples were hard. The way my shirt was wrinkled and wet, it was apparent I had been grabbling and twisting my nipples.

While groping and caressing my body, tilting my head back ever so slightly because of the stimulating treatment I was giving myself, I watched the zipper to the tent finish its way across the bottom and begin moving up the right side of the entrance. As I watched the zipper moving, I reached into my now sweaty, sticky undershorts and pulled out my throbbing cock. I couldn't help it. I had to have my dick in my hands. My entire body felt flushed and euphoric. My feet and hands were tingling. My dick was dripping precum with every throb and bounce it made.

I quickly shoved my thumbs behind the waistband of my undershorts and slowly pulled them down, lower and lower on my hips. My dick was straining against the fabric of my shorts. I kept pulling as I watched the zipper on the tent move. The friction rubbing against my smoldering cock was almost unbearable. As the zipper to the entrance of the tint moved upward, I continued sliding my underwear down. Suddenly, my throbbing cock jumped up and out from behind my shorts. My dick banged against my rock-hard abs. Precum glistened in the sunlight as it splattered against my treasure trail and dripped onto my pubes. I wrapped the waistband of my undershorts under my low-hanging balls. This made all 11 inches of my thick dick stand straight out, at full attention. Every breath I took or movement would make my dick bounce almost like it was on a spring. I spit a thick puddle of drool in my hand and rubbed it into the sticky piss slit of my dick. The callouses on my fingers and hands felt like rough, weathered leather embedded with pins and needles as I continued working myself into an uncontrollable frenzy.

The zipper to the tent was now making its way across the top of the opening.

Like a football player, I crouched and bent my shoulders toward the ground, ready for a scrimmage. I was standing near the entrance to the tent, dick in my hand, wearing my work boots, heavy wool socks, tighty-whities, and my gold polo work shirt. A clear strand of pre-cum dripped from the head of my dick. I reached down, wiped it on my fingers, brought them to my lips, and sucked. I swear it felt like I had stepped on a live electrical wire because I have never experienced shocks like the ones coursing through my body. The taste of my precum was like a bittersweet mix of salt and sugar on my tongue, and I became ravenous for that flavor.

As I moved toward the tent, I stepped out of and over my khaki shorts as if they weren't even there. I positioned my solid body right in front of the entrance to the tent, maintaining control over who could go into or come out of the tent. My dick was merely inches away from brushing against the canvas of that door flap. I could even feel the warmth of the sun-warmed canvas of the tent wafting over my throbbing, dripping cock.

As soon as the door flap on the tent opened and fell away from the opening, I saw Brent standing there, sweat running down his brow, dripping off his nose, and landing on his mustache-covered upper lip. He leaned left to glance through the door as he pulled the flap back, trying to discern what was happening outside the tent.

I couldn't control myself. When Brent began pulling the door flap back, I was hit with a hot, wet, salty, and sweaty man scent inside the tent. The storm we had recently had, and the fact that the tent had been closed up in the rain and humidity and now the heat, did nothing but create an oven of man scents.

Brent looked so innocent, standing there with his muscles bulging in his uniform and sweat running down his furry arms and face. As soon as the flap was pulled all the way open, I saw Brent's shocked expression as he noticed I was standing there with my huge throbbing cock in my hand, stroking it and leering in his direction.

Brent's jaw dropped, and his eyes widened. I don't know if he was more shocked that I was standing in front of him, seminude, or if it was because of the superhuman size of my 11" cock.

With the heat emanating from the connection between my dick and my hand as I stroked up a sweat, I made eye contact with him; I saw a flash of awareness cross his face. Brent, somehow, anticipated what he thought was about to happen based on what he saw, and he vowed he would fight to prevent it.

Brent was no dummy. He loved watching porn. He also loved watching a kinkier form of bondage or rape-type materials. He quickly studied my face, and the look in my eye reminded him of the looks he'd seen in the eyes of guys raping women in those videos he loved to watch.

Brent moved quickly and attempted to unroll and push the door flap to the tent back into place so he could connect the zipper and close the tent back up. I'm sure Brent knew there would be no way to keep me out of the tent forever if he successfully closed the opening, but he had to know it was only a matter of time before I would get into that tent.

Brent was strong and quick, but I had strength plus endurance, and I was pretty darned fast on my feet as well. Without warning, I lunged forward, firmly placing one foot inside the tent. Brent groaned, yelled, and pushed the flap against me. The unzipped edges of the flap came into contact with my throbbing bouncing cock. The rough feeling of the warm canvas caressing and scratching my wet dick was forcing me to pant, growl, and moan.

I pushed against the canvas flap and sent Brent stumbling back into the tent. Brent could not secure the zipper connection, so closing the door flap was pointless.

Feeling Brent's hard body, even behind that canvas flap, sent my body into overdrive. My dick was throbbing and bouncing. I was getting off feeling the rough canvas tent fabric fighting with my dick. My underwear was tight enough to wrap the waistband under my low-hanging balls and stay that way.

Suddenly, as a surge of testosterone raced through my body, I grabbed the collar of my work shirt, growled loudly, and began pulling. I could hear the fabric of my shirt start to rip and tear. I flexed my arms, chest, and shoulders, and the material gave way.

Brent continued backing away from me and into the tent. He stepped over to his sleeping quarters and tried to unfurl and secure that door flap. I lunged toward him again. I had to feel him. I wanted to feel his breath on my skin. As Brent continued trying to get the flap down to give him even the slightest protection from me, I knew it was time to pounce upon my prey. I slapped the canvas door flap out of Brent's hands. He had a startled and almost fearful look in his eyes. I caught Brent's shirt as the canvas flap swung out of Brent's grasp.

Brent continued trying to pull away from me, and I held fast to his shirt. As Brent pulled, I heard his shirt beginning to rip. I held on tightly and yanked the front of his shirt down and toward me. As I did, I listened to his shirt tear again, which came completely off in my hands. Brent continued backing away from me. As he did so, I noticed his fantastic body. Brent was backing up, alarmed, and all of the muscles in his chest, shoulders, and arms were flexing as he defensively tried to escape my advances.

I was drooling while looking at the nice dusting of fur all over Brent's chest, especially that darker, thicker tuft of hair growing between his muscled pecs. Brent was panting, and his breath was ragged. I could see his ab muscles flexing with every breath. He had his hands and arms thrown out in front of him in a defensive stance.

As he backed away, I kept getting whiffs of his sweaty, musky odor. The bittersweet smell of Brent's sweaty pits and the dampness of the hair on his chest made my dick throb with every beat of my racing heart. I slapped my dick. That sent shockwaves into the deepest recesses of my groin.

I had to touch, feel, and molest Brent's body. I aimed to possess this hot, sexy man by stroking his flesh and worshipping his sweaty manliness. I vowed to own this man, and he would thank me. I lunged forward again and grabbed Brent's forearms. I was stronger than he. I don't know if the added strength resulted from the strange mosquito bites or if it was adrenaline, but I pushed Brent backward until his back was up against the wall, separating his sleeping area from Roger's.

Brent yelled, "NO! STOP!"

He said, "Tom, Tom, what's the matter with you."

I continued holding him tightly. From a bit of wrestling experience from my youth and general fighting experience, I quickly threw Brent's hands and arms down toward his sides. As I did this, I lunged again and wrapped him in a huge bear hug.

I could feel Brent's hard, sweaty body against mine. I could smell his salty sweat. I could smell the bitterness of his armpits. I was face-to-face with Brent. He was trying not to look me in the eye, but as close as our faces were, he couldn't escape me.

Brent was breathing heavily and struggling to break my embrace. Each time he breathed in and exhaled, the whiskers over his upper lip that formed his sexy mustache would ruffle, and I could hear what sounded like a puff of air.

I could feel Brent's body tensing as he struggled.

Brent yelled again, "GET THE FUCK OFF OF ME!"

I was rabid. I pushed against Brent, backed up slightly, and body-slammed him. The fabric wall dividing Brent's sleeping quarters from Roger's finally gave way. As the fabric wall fell, so did Brent and I. I fell on top of him. We rolled once, but I pushed as we moved and fell back on top of Brent again.

Brent continued struggling, kicking his hairy legs against mine. Each movement he made would cause his hips, legs, and crotch to brush up against my throbbing cock.

I was on top of him. He looked at me again. I stared deeply into his eyes. He suddenly stopped kicking and struggling. Maybe he thought if he tried to reason with me gently, he could still keep anything terrible from happening.

Brent's eyes moved left and right, focusing on my left and right eyes and back again. As quickly as I had been upon him, I dipped my head toward his. He got a look of panic in his eyes and tried to move his head sideways to avoid facing me. I had his arms pinned behind his back now. I was lying on top of him. I outweighed Brent by about 30 pounds, which was definitely to my advantage.

As I continued lying on top of Brent, I reached up and grabbed the back of his head and began pulling his head toward mine. Brent strained and struggled to keep the distance between our faces. I continued pulling him toward me. Brent's breath became more ragged. He was shaking and trying to pull away.

Suddenly, our lips brushed together. I could smell the stale coffee on his breath. Brent's breath was heavy and moist. He struggled again to break free, and I quickly grasped his head and forced my mouth onto his. He tried to keep his lips together but was no match for my sex-crazed state. I pushed, and suddenly Brent's lips and jaw gave way, and my tongue was deep inside his mouth, swabbing every surface I could find.

Brent struggled again and again. I could feel the hot air escaping from his nose as I continued raping his mouth with mine. He was destined to suffocate if he didn't breathe through his mouth. Brent had no choice. I held him in a tight embrace. I continued invading his mouth with my tongue, and I began grinding my dick against the crotch of his shorts.

Brent seemed to calm down and relax, but it was only a ploy of his to try and get away from me. As Brent seemed to stop struggling, I relaxed my grip on him. Once Brent was aware that I was distracted by him not putting up a fight, he surprised me, got one arm free, pushed against my head and shoulder, and rolled me off of him.

I was shocked, but for only a minute. Brent crawled over and away from me, trying to get to the other side of the tent. He limped and dragged himself out of my embrace, but I was too quick.

I quickly jumped up and hopped a couple of feet over, and as Brent tried to crawl past me, I grabbed the waist of his shorts and yanked hard. The thin fabric of his shorts and his muscular weight were no match. I could hear material slowly ripping, and with a hard tug, I pulled Brent's shorts off him. This left Brent with his work boots, socks, and what looked like military silkies for underwear.

As Brent's body was increasingly exposed, my sexual desire to overpower, control, and sexually own increased. I climbed on top of Brent, then body slammed against him as he struggled and tried to crawl like soldiers were trained to do when navigating barbed wire fencing on the combat field, but this attempt failed as I was able to knock the wind out of him for a few seconds, allowing me just enough time to quickly grab the seam of his undershorts and rip them away from his furry ass crack. Brent's hairy ass cheeks bounced as the fabric of his undershorts ripped away.

As Brent was still trying to recover from the last body slam, I quickly split open his ass cheeks and spit. I spit again.

Both times, a nice, thick, wet glop of saliva landed on Brent's tight pink rosebud. Brent's struggles did nothing more than cause his ass crack and butthole to gyrate such that the spit I had delivered began to grind its way deeper into his hole.

Brent reached around to wipe his butt, but I grabbed his hands and smacked them again. Brent grunted and bounced his hips, trying to get me off him. He was still weak from the previous body slam.

I raised quickly and slammed him again. When I'd slam into him, the feeling of his rock-hard body under me was like someone taking a hot molten hammer and hitting it deep into my loins. I wanted to share that heat with this hot, studly body below. This added body slam knocked the breath out of Brent again.

Brent lay on his stomach, dazed, panting, and trying to catch his breath. I could feel the wetness of his sweaty body as he lay under me. As Brent lay still, trying to regain consciousness, I quickly spit all over my dick, spit again into his tight ass, and remounted him.

Brent came to and, once again, tried to buck me off. This time, I was well prepared. I placed an arm over the back of his neck and held his face against the tent's floor. I used my hairy, muscled legs and forcefully spread Brent's legs apart. This helped to expose Brent's tight pink hole.

Brent moaned, "NO, please, Tom, no, what are you doing."

I was a madman. I ignored Brent's cries.

I hocked another load of spit into the palm of my hand, wrapped it around my dick, slicked my throbbing dick, and began moving toward Brent's pink virgin hole. Brent kept shaking and struggling, but I could tell the fight in him had started to weaken. Each time Brent tried to move, his efforts seemed weak and tired.

I could tell that Brent felt the head of my dick rubbing his tight, muscled, furry ass cheeks because I could feel him trying to flex his ass to try and squeeze me out of his hairy crack. I saw another sticky strand of precum smear itself over Brent's ass crack and stick his ass hairs together as my dick continued to belch more and more sticky juices. Brent continued to wiggle his ass and hips back and forth haphazardly. His movements no longer felt like they were being made in protest but were more likely rocking motions of him trying to prepare for the worst mentally.

Brent's furry ass bumping and grinding against my body reignited the fires inside me, almost like a match being struck in a room full of gasoline. I could feel the flashes racing through me, and my dick jumped and spit and pushed deeper into Brent's ass crack.

Brent stopped struggling altogether. It appeared he was trying to assess his options. But he was still making no effort to try and get away or throw me off of him anymore.

As I slowly began pushing the thick head of my throbbing cock against Brent's cherry hole, I could feel his hole trying to keep me out. I almost wanted to tell Brent that each time his cherry hole squeezed and brushed against the head of my dick, that was almost like French kissing my dick, and that just made me want to be deep inside him that much more, but I didn't share this with him. I focused more on getting my dick inside Brent's hot hole. I kept telling myself that once I was inside that hot hole, all the burning pain I was experiencing would subside.

Brent moaned and began wiggling and bucking again. The head of my dick started feeling the ring of Brent's ass giving away. It felt like a thick rubber band was slowly being rolled over the head of my dick and down the shaft toward my balls. As I kept pushing, I leaned over onto Brent from behind. My mouth was at his right ear. My breath was ragged, but I leaned in, licked his ear, nibbled the area of his neck just behind his ear, and whispered, "You want this; you know you do. This is good for you and me. This is team building 101 right here."

Brent's entire body stiffened. Every sinew and muscle in his body stiffened. I could feel Brent's ass lips still trying to keep me out, but me and my dick were persistent, and I continued pushing and pushing. Brent raised his head back toward mine from behind. I felt his hips gyrate once or twice, and suddenly my dick began to sink deeper into his tight hole, almost like a sinking ship that reaches that point of no return and begins to slide under the ocean surface, moving faster and faster. Brent's ass muscles had given up.

Finally, I buried myself inside Brent's hole. I felt his tight ass cheeks pinching and gyrating as my bushy pubes brushed deep into his sweaty ass crack. I pulled my dick halfway out of his hole. Brent sucked in the air, and his body shook. I slowly pushed back into his ass. This time I could hear my balls slap against Brent's ass.

Brent whimpered and panted and tried to say, "Please, no, please don't do......this....please, Tom.......please stop."

As Brent continued to protest, I found that each time he said something like this, it made me harder and hornier. Each time Brent would beg me to stop, I would push deeper and harder into him, jabbing his spasming hole and feeling the warm tug on my dick as I shoved my dick in and out of his chute.

In no time, we developed a rhythm. Brent had given up struggling. I don't know if he enjoyed being raped, but I don't think he hated it. Off and on, Brent's hips would jerk up and meet the pounding I was giving him from behind. I could then drive my dick even deeper into his sloppy hole.

As our rhythm continued, Brent raised his head again, arched his back, and as I slammed my throbbing cock deep into his hole, he leaned back and positioned his head so our lips were close together again, and our beards and mustaches rubbed and brushed together. Suddenly, Brent stuck his tongue out and reached for my mouth. I gladly covered Brent's mouth with my own, and we began ravaging one another again.

As we continued our passionate manly kisses, Brent said, "Please stop; please don't do this." But his comments were deceiving because Brent had begun rocking his hips harder and harder. This kept helping my dick thrust deeper and deeper into his hole.

I leaned over at one point, spit into Brent's mouth, buried my tongue deep down his throat, and thrust my cock to the base. Brent screamed out. I could feel his body convulsing and realized that Brent was shooting his load all over the tent floor while I was still deep inside, pounding his hole, quickly changing the fact that he was an anal virgin to him becoming an anal slut, my slut.

Brent's body continued to convulse. His ass muscles were throbbing and pinching in unison with the thrusts of his orgasm. At one point, Brent's ass muscles clamped onto my throbbing dick and held me tightly inside him. I had never experienced this kind of feeling, not with anyone. I thought my dick would rip off my groin because the pressure of Brent clamping and holding my dick was earth-shattering.

As Brent lay on the floor, his ass muscles milking my throbbing cock and his tongue fighting battles with mine as our mouths linked together like conjoined twins, I felt the telltale rush coming from my loins. One more jiggle of Brent's asshole surrounded my hard cock, and I suddenly began shooting my load deeply into his ass.

I grunted, groaned, and moaned. I involuntarily ground and pounded my ejaculating dick into the deepest recesses of Brent's tight hairy hole. I could feel the pressure building inside Brent's ass chute as I filled it full of my spunk and rapidly filled up the void inside his ass to the point where it started pushing my dick out. I quickly shoved my cock deep inside Brent's ass again.

Brent thrust his hips back to meet my thrusts and shouted, "FUUUUCK!!!!"

My dick kept ejaculating and pulsing, and Brent's ass muscles kept milking.

As our lustful behavior subsided, I slowly pulled my thick cock out of Brent's ass. Several times I felt him try to hold onto my dick with his ass muscles.

I finally felt my dick exit Brent's ass with a loud, sloppy popping sound.

Brent reached up and caressed my arms as I wrapped them around him. He leaned up against me again, and we kissed. This time, the kiss seemed more genuine.

Neither Brent nor I were aware that although receiving bites from those "KWEER Skeeters" could turn any straight man into a gay whore, another side effect of this strange anomaly was that any infected man's cum was also lethal, and injecting it into another man would slowly but surely cause that man to have gay tendencies.

It would come out later during an investigation that if an infected person didn't continue to have sex with others, injecting and sharing their tainted jism orally or anally, or did not come into contact with any further mosquito bites, the rampant sex drive they had experienced and the need to bury their burning dicks and inject their unholy seed into another warm body would fade. But that's another story to tell.

Now that Brent's ass was full of my spunk, a slow conversion was happening inside his psyche. Suddenly, the thought of having sex with someone of the same gender was of no consequence. It was the overwhelming desire to experience an orgasm that had never been encountered, and a new burning desire that drove the infected individual to seek as much sex as possible to continue to share this addictive and mind-blowing type of orgasm they had never dreamed existed.

I rolled over onto my side and brought Brent with me. He gladly rolled, and we were spooning me behind him, my furry arms wrapped around him, smelling the sweat and sex on both of our bodies. I allowed my hand to fall over Brent's dick gently. I could feel his dick jump and pulse again. I felt Brent's dick jump, and my dick jumped, swelled again, and pressed against Brent's ass crack. I could feel dried cum on Brent's ass rubbing against the head of my cock.

Chapter Fifteen

I heard footsteps west of the campsite as Brent and I held our tingling bodies in a tight bear hug. It sounded like someone was running. Brent and I jumped up, and realizing we had destroyed our clothing, we each grabbed our shower towels and wrapped them around our waists.

As the footsteps slowed, we heard Roger yell, "Hey, Tom, Brent, are you there?"

From the urgent tone of Roger's voice, it sounded like something wasn't right. Brent and I came out of the sleeping tent. Even though we had just shared earth-shattering orgasms, Brent and my dicks were still semi-hard and tingling. There was a bulge behind each of our towels.

As we left the tent, Roger came around the corner and stopped. He looked at both of us, looked at the towels wrapped around our waists, and said, "Um…what's going on here?"

Brent and I laughed and said we weren't sure when he and Cliff would be back and had decided we were both going to take a shower. Roger nodded as if he understood, but I could still detect a strange look in his eyes, like he didn't believe everything we told him.

Had Roger shown up a few minutes earlier, it would have been doubly hard for Brent or me to hide that we had just had the hottest sex we'd ever had, and it wasn't with the opposite sex, like usual.

Roger still seemed aloof but stood facing us and appeared agitated. He rocked from one foot to the other. He said, "Cliff and I ran into trouble while in the field today."

I was immediately alarmed and could tell that Brent was also upset. I grabbed Roger's shoulder and asked, "What happened?"

As Roger explained what had transpired after they had weathered that freak thunderstorm, I kept my hand on Roger's back and began absentmindedly running my hand lower and lower.

Roger described the camouflage netting, the booby trap, the moonshine still, the two men, and Cliff's fate. Roger also tried to explain about the strange mosquitoes he had seen. He kept stopping, scratching his head, and telling us he didn't understand what he saw at times because it seemed like Cliff was enjoying what was happening to him, and yet Roger thought it appeared Cliff was being held against his will and was being raped. Roger kept saying he couldn't focus on what made him uncomfortable about the events, but things seemed weird.

Roger continued talking about dodging the "Skeeters" as they flew away from him and asked if we had seen or heard those strange insects here at the camp since it appeared they were coming in this direction.

At about this time, Brent moved over to Roger's other side, placed his hand on Roger's shoulder, and began caressing his back. Brent said, "Damn, this sounds awful; we must get over there and help Cliff."

As Brent said this, he and I ran our hands down Roger's back. I was mesmerized while looking at Roger and noting the flame red-orange color of his head and body hair. It was apparent Roger was a "ginger," but I hadn't previously noticed how hot it made me feel to look at that red fuzz on his head, arms, neck, and face. As I listened to him talk, I wondered if his pubes were the same color.

I caressed Roger's back and would say, "Uh Hum, Yes," or "WOW," as he spoke. All the while, Brent and I were subtly bumping our fingers together behind Roger's back as we both caressed him. On one of our successive caressing moves, Brent's fingers and mine automatically interlocked as our arms wrapped around Roger's waist, and we pulled him close to us.

Roger stopped talking. I ran my hand down his red, furry, muscled forearm and told him we'd get over to help Cliff. The feeling of the thick course ginger fur on Roger's arm as I rubbed it sent shockwaves through my groin again. I could feel the sweat from Roger's shirt rubbing against my bare torso. I could feel Roger's body pushing closer into my body and realized that was because Brent was subtly pushing against Roger, causing him to be squeezed between us.

Roger said, "Hey, um, we don't need to be this close," he attempted to pull away from us. Brent grabbed Roger's other arm and caressed it. Brent's fingers continued to stay intertwined with mind at Roger's lower back.

As Roger started trying to move away from us, we increased the squeeze between our bodies. Brent leaned over toward Roger and sniffed his shirt. I leaned over and suddenly wanted to stick my tongue into Roger's ear and clean his lobes well. I leaned closer to Roger's ear and began blowing hot breath at the back of his neck.

Roger immediately pushed away. He stepped back and looked at me and Brent. He glanced down at our crotches, and that's when I looked at Brent, then his crotch, and noticed Brent was looking at my crotch as well. I looked down and noted I was rock hard and throbbing under my towel, and it appeared Brent was in the same boat.

Roger shook his head and said, "FUCK....what the fuck is happening. Get the fuck away from me, you fucking faggots." He took a few more steps back, and Brent and I advanced in his direction. Roger yelled again, "I'm warning you, stay the fuck away from me."

I didn't care how much of a fight Roger wanted to put up; I was returning to my overheated sexual desires again, and I wanted that ginger stud. I moved toward Roger.

Brent was wiping drool from his lips. He grinned at me and took another step toward Roger. Roger looked at Brent, jumped, looked back at me again, jumped one more step back, turned, and took off running.

Although Brent and I could easily have run after Roger, our brains were still tainted with infection, and we were mad to find more hot bodies to feed a newfound urgency to penetrate and molest over and over again. Having explained what had happened at the moonshine camp with Cliff, Roger had alerted us that Cliff needed our help.

Sure, we had turned into voracious sex hunters, but we still had enough wits about us to know that we needed to help Cliff because he was part of our team. Therefore, Brent and I decided to deal with Roger later, but Cliff's predicament was more serious.

Brent and I both threw on a new pair of shorts. I didn't need to throw on a full uniform of clothing. It was too hot, and my body was too hot, and that wasn't just from the day's heat. Brent and I came out of the damaged sleeping tent wearing cargo shorts, work boots, and ballcaps.

I leaned toward Brent and looked him in the eyes. Brent tilted his head up, and our lips connected again. Our mouths fought a battle of lust that only two hot horny beings could fight. There were no winners, but each party enjoyed the struggle that ensued.

I slapped Brent's ass, felt the muscle bounce, and said, "Let's go get our, boy."

Brent twisted my nipple, slapped my ass, and said, "OK, Boss, let's hit it."

We took off heading toward the moonshine still Roger had described and figured that because we were briskly walking west, we'd make good time because we were not surveying anything, only walking to find our teammate. In approximately an hour and a half, we finally came to the two stands of trees described by Roger and where Cliff and Roger's adventure had begun.

While Brent and I were working toward the moonshine campsite, Roger ran to escape us. Brent and I were undoubtedly under the influence of whatever those "Skeeters" had done to us, so what seemed normal to us did not seem normal to Roger.

Considering Roger had seen the strange goings on at the moonshine campsite, those peculiar insects, and then seeing Brent and me acting strangely, he decided it best to try and get back to the main road and see if he could contact the authorities. Unfortunately, because Roger had panicked and ran out of the survey team's campsite so quickly, he had not thought to stop for any supplies or equipment. As he ran through the forested, swampy area, he realized he had not even thought about grabbing keys for one of the company trucks and driving himself to the authorities. He also hadn't thought to grab a radio or compass.

'*Damn it,*' Roger thought. From his hunting experiences, he knew that being unprepared and not having the proper equipment could become a death sentence out in the wild. He figured he was going to have to take his chances. Roger figured, worst case scenario, he would get to the main road and keep walking until he came to some form of civilization.

Chapter Sixteen

State Trooper Officer Richard Plitt was bored. He was part of the State of Florida's program to install a state-level enforcement officer throughout the various counties to help show a local and state-level interest in helping fight crime and maintain law and order. He had been assigned to patrol a very remote area of the wetlands that fell inside his county of jurisdiction. Occasionally, one of the rookies would have to pull this boring, routine shift.

Officer Plitt had been on this tour of duty before. He knew there was little to no action, and all he did was drive around wasting gas and putting unnecessary mileage on his patrol car. He smirked and thought, *'I guess I'm not paying for this, so it's just a job.'*

He was shocked when he saw a young man run out onto the road waving his hands as he rounded the corner on a remote road near one of the wetlands, including federal land reserves. As his cruiser pulled closer to the young man, the guy stopped waving his hands. Officer Plitt stopped his cruiser. He radioed to headquarters that he was stopping to aid a distressed citizen. He couldn't name the cross streets where he was located but gave a general description of his whereabouts. An acknowledgment came back quickly.

As Office Plitt cradled his radio, he grabbed his nightstick and the hat that went along with his uniform. He exited the cruiser, placed the nightstick into the holster on his large work belt, and walked over to where Roger was anxiously standing at the side of the road.

Officer Plitt was a strapping young man. He was 28 and would be turning 29 at the end of this year. He had grown up near this area but had moved away to Ft Lauderdale when he went to college and subsequently applied for and obtained his certification as a Florida State Trooper. He has been a state trooper for three years now. Unfortunately, with this new statewide program, he did have to supplement his shifts with these random "state-sanctioned" tasks. He usually was busy tracking speeders on the interstate or investigating local crimes. So, the occasional assignment to sit or drive around and look at endless miles of swamp and marshlands was okay as long as it happened very sporadically.

Officer Plitt (Richard, as most of his friends and family called him) had been a star on the track team at both his high school and later during his college career. He had won several trophies and awards for his speed and agility. Richard kept his dark ginger hair in a strict military high and tight style. He had a huge, bushy red mustache that grew over his top lip, softening the severity of his upper lip but seeming to highlight the angular sharpness of his manly jawline. The rest of his face was shaved clean to abide by the rules and regulations set forth by the state of Florida for enforcement personnel. Richard stood at 6' 3" tall. He weighed a healthy 210 of pure fat-free muscle.

Although Richard had spent most of his athletic career in track and field, where being toned, fit, and possessing agility were the main factors to winning championships, now that he was no longer an actual "athlete," Richard focused more on hitting the weights, packing on some extra muscle, and giving up that slender, toned, sinewy physical appearance he had had since high school. So far, he'd been lucky to gain about 30 additional pounds of muscle.

It was apparent Richard had been in the process of transforming his body because the standard taupe State Trooper's uniform he was wearing looked like it was about to pop every seam or button because he had been packing on muscle and had yet to go in for a fitting to update his uniforms to fit that bulkier but fitter body he was creating.

Richard got out of the cruiser and walked over to Roger. Roger seemed jittery. Richard kept his cool and decided to keep his distance and try to find out what was happening. As he walked toward Roger, Roger stepped toward him. Richard placed his hand on his pistol and said, "Stop, that's far enough."

Roger stopped walking forward. As he stood, he said, "Officer, please help me. Something is going on out here, and it's not right."

Officer Plitt continued to approach Roger cautiously. He asked, "What are you talking about? Can you please describe the situation?"

As Richard stood facing Roger, Roger began to recant his story. He described what he had seen on the neighboring property. He explained how strange the men he had encountered all seemed to suddenly turn into some wild animals who appeared to be hunting one another for sex, and it wasn't typical sex but men actively pursuing other men to have sex with.

Richard tried to believe Roger's story, but he was still skeptical. He thought, *'There is no such thing as a straight man suddenly turning gay or having gay tendencies without some cause.'*

Roger continued explaining. He described the strange mosquitoes he had seen. He said he'd seen them stinging the others, drastically changing their actions and attitudes.

As Roger continued explaining, Richard subconsciously assessed him. Based on Roger's body movements, speech, eyes, etc., Richard was confident Roger was not on drugs or drunk or anything like that. It would not be noticeable if he were on something without performing a drug or sobriety test. Roger seemed to be an average strapping young man with a fascinating story.

Richard finally calmed Roger down and said, "Why don't we head over to this moonshine still you've described and talk to the people there."

Roger seemed timid about doing this but agreed that with the Trooper there with him, he felt much safer than trying to handle this himself. Roger decided to climb into the cruiser, and they would head down the road to investigate.

As the police cruiser moved down the remote road, the sound of a thousand old electric guitar strings screeching could suddenly be heard. Officer Plitt slowed the car and said, "Do you hear that?"

Roger nodded and explained that this was the sound those strange mosquitoes were making, and he saw a thick patch of those green bugs flying toward the cruiser. The windshield was splattered with lime green splotches as the cruiser and the "skeeters" collided. The green splatters glowed in the sunlight as the bugs were smashed against the windshield.

Richard slammed on the brakes and abruptly stopped the cruiser. He and Roger watched as the glowing green slime dribbled down the windshield. Roger turned toward Richard and said, "I wasn't lying." Richard, both hands on the steering wheel, mouth agape, just nodded, and they began to move forward again, slowly getting closer to the area where the moonshine still was located.

Finally, only after a few minutes, Officer Plitt and Roger pulled up to a clearing along the road. There were two pickup trucks parked in this clearing. Roger saw the trucks and said he had not come this far along the road to notice them earlier but that this was where he had seen the still and the two guys raping his coworker.

As they pulled up to the site and parked a little way up and over the hill, what looked like some engine or pump station appeared. There were tubes, pipes, and barrels all connected. Richard thought, '*This was no random pile of metal. This was put together with purpose.*'

Roger quickly pointed out the still and said, "That's where I saw everything I've described." Officer Plitt finally started to believe some of what Roger had been telling him.

Being the dutiful law officer, Officer Plitt advised Roger to remain in the cruiser and that he would investigate. There was no reason for him to get involved or injured along with his workmate. Roger nodded in agreement but kept looking over the hill toward the still.

Plitt donned his hat, grabbed his nightstick, and exited the police cruiser. He crouched lower, and with his hand hovering over his holstered gun, he meticulously moved toward that tangled mass of pipes and tubes. Plitt's tight state trooper uniform was stretching and bending with his every move. As he crested the hill overlooking the moonshine still, he could see a man hanging in some strange roped apparatus. The guy was naked, and Officer Plitt thought it appeared he was hard, and the ropes were tied so that they encircled his dick and balls and seemed to hold it upright away from the captive's body very tightly.

Plitt decided to move closer so he could more clearly see what was going on and be able to make his report. His balls tingled with the thought that, if nothing else, he might have discovered another one of those moonshine still operations that need to be put to rest for good. He was already hearing the adoring crowd cheer him as he received the award for excellently arresting more criminals. He took a few steps closer and could see much more clearly.

As Officer Plitt crouched low in the brush, he looked, blinked, rubbed his eyes, and looked again. The guy hanging in this roped thing was accompanied by two more hairy, muscled, swarthy-looking guys. These guys had the appearance of rough swampland trade. Rough around the edges and scruffy, but muscular and able to put in a man's worth of work at any given job they chose. The strange thing was that all three men he was viewing were naked, and they all had hard-ons. As Plitt continued looking, it appeared the two rougher guys were kissing, licking, and fondling the guy who was tied up. The surprising thing was that it appeared the victim was responding to the fondling, kissing, and caressing by arching his body and swinging so that he could brush against the other men.

Officer Plitt was okay with all sexual orientations. He didn't even care if people were doing nasty things out here in the wild, but he was concerned for public safety, so if what Roger had told him was true, why was Roger's workmate seemingly going along with his tormentors? He continued watching.

Marcus and Pete were still at the height of their "skeeter" infections, and there was no letting off of the hot waves of passion still flowing through their bodies. They were kissing, licking, caressing, and fondling their prey, and Cliff, their game, was responding to every touch. No one knew they were being watched at the top of the hill.

Neither Marcus nor Pete seemed to make any attempt to loosen or remove Cliff's bindings. And Cliff seemed content to hang and feel his body being worshipped repeatedly.

Officer Plitt was working out his plan of attack and was deep in thought while continuing his surveillance and hadn't heard Brent and me creeping up from behind. We were at a location just out of view from the parking area down the hill, so there would have been no way for Roger to see us, and Roger would have already lost sight of Officer Plitt.

I stepped on a branch, and Officer Plitt suddenly jumped up and grabbed for his police revolver. Brent and I both put our hands up in the air, then our fingers to our lips as if to advise we be quiet, and then I whispered to Officer Plitt that we were part of the survey party and we were here to investigate the same story Roger had shared with us.

I could see Officer Plitt calm, and his body movements relaxed. I did notice the blood in my dick start to fill again as I started noticing how tight that taupe-colored state trooper's uniform fitted over this young officer's body. Officer Plitt had a nice V-taper. He had broad shoulders, a hard bulging chest, and all that narrowed to a slim, tight waist. I could see the familiar outline of his ass pressing against the seat of his law enforcement uniform. His pants were so tight I could see the outline where his boxer briefs rested underneath his trousers along the middle of his thick thighs.

As I approached Officer Plitt, I noticed Brent move up to his other side. I felt that telltale sign that the sexual juices in my body were churning again. Whatever coursed through my veins was relentless, pushing my libido and sexual organs into overdrive. As I glanced across Officer Plitt, I noticed that the front of Brent's shorts was beginning to swell. I could see Brent's thickening cockhead begin to snake down the left leg of his shorts.

Seeing Brent's hard-on growing only fueled the fire again burning inside me. I could smell the cologne mixed with sweat from this man-of-the-law as the breeze whipped around us. As I returned my gaze to Officer Plitt, I noticed he was glancing down at Brent's crotch as well. Officer Plitt raised his hand under his trooper hat and scratched his head as if confused about what he was seeing and experiencing.

Officer Plitt suddenly turned his head and was shocked that I was staring in his direction. I made eye contact and stared deeply into his eyes, only for a few seconds. I grunted, cleared my throat, and said, "Maybe we should head down there and see what's going on? I want to make sure my fellow employee is all right."

Officer Plitt stared back at me; his hand was still resting on the revolver in its holster, but his body language told me he was calm and collected. He glanced down the hill toward the three men below us and nodded.

Brent stepped closer to Officer Plitt, patted him on the shoulder, and said, "Let's go check this out." And we nudged the trooper and slowly and quietly moved down the hill.

As we came to the clearing of the moonshine encampment, we could hear moans, groans, and slurping sounds. The culprits making the noises were so engrossed in their simmering sexual actions that they weren't even aware we were there.

Marcus and Pete were rubbing their naked bodies all over Cliff. Cliff was moaning, and his dick was bouncing, and every so often, one of the other brother's hairy legs would brush against Cliff's cock and send shockwaves through his body. He would react by jerking and sensually rocking his body, wanting more and more contact.

As we approached this group of writhing men, I was beginning to find it hard to control my feelings. I wanted to be in the middle of that group of men, one of them my employee, working one another over, licking, kissing, spitting, sucking, fucking, and repeating. My dick began to spring to life inside my shorts. I, again, glanced over to Brent and saw he had released the top button of his shorts, and the bulge in those shorts was so hard that you could make out separate outlines of his dick and his balls. Brent was absentmindedly rubbing his right nipple and would occasionally close his eyes and tip his head back just a little. As I continued to watch this, I glanced down and realized I had been massaging my left nipple.

Brent moved closer to Officer Plitt, and I involuntarily moved toward him. I could smell the state trooper's sweaty, musky scent. Suddenly, my nose was assaulted by the more pungent smell of the three men we watched.

Brent touched Officer Plitt's lower back and slowly pushed forward. As Brent and the trooper slowly began to move forward, I fell into step with them as we approached the other three men.

Cliff suddenly raised his head, glanced in our direction with his glazed eyes, sneered, and said, "DAMN, there are those hot fucking studs I work with."

Immediately, Marcus and Pete turned their heads in surprise. No sooner did they see us than they lunged in our direction.

Officer Plitt was shoved to the ground, and when he fell, he dragged Brent along with him. I would have remained standing had I not suddenly been knocked to the ground when Marcus slammed into me. As I tried to roll away, I could see Pete wrestling with Brent, but Brent had Pete in an armlock, and they were both on top of Officer Plitt, who appeared to be pinned and helpless.

The scuffle continued. The sound of boots, feet, clothing, and flesh scraping against the dusty ground could be heard together with grunts and groans as each man tried to overpower the other.

As the fight continued, suddenly Marcus began massaging my hard cock. Marcus seemed to be a strong man. I'm pretty damned strong, but he could hold me down no matter what I tried. As he continued to hold me, I could feel his sweaty legs pressing against mine. My dick strained in my shorts, but Marcus was still naked from his last sexual escapade. I could feel his throbbing cock bang and press against my crotch as he finally straddled me and forced my arms over my head as I lay on my back. Marcus began scooting toward my head as I was being held in position. I could see the veins popping on his muscled, hairy thighs as the sweat continued to glisten, and I even saw droplets of sweat forming in his massive pubic patch.

As I struggled against Marcus's advances, part of me began to give in. The "skeeter" infection was still coursing through my body, and the added body contact stirred my inner juices. Marcus took advantage of my relaxed state and approached my face. Before I could take another breath, my mouth was opened, and Marcus's throbbing cock was rammed into my mouth as it was buried to the base, and his pubes covered my mouth and nose. At first, I couldn't breathe. All I saw was black curly fur. All I could smell was sweat, dried cum, and piss. Marcus wiggled his hips and kept burying his dick down my throat.

Just when I thought I would pass out, Marcus pulled back, allowing me to gasp for air. No sooner had I gotten a breath of air than Marcus shoved his dick back down my throat. Marcus began pulling out, pushing in, reaching down, and grabbing my throbbing crotch. He grinned an evil grin as he looked me in the eye and made it apparent he knew that I knew that we both wanted this hot, filthy man-sex.

As Marcus assaulted my mouth, Brent used his old wrestling training and quickly overtook Pete. Brent quickly got behind Pete and put him in a deadlock with Pete's hands held behind his neck. As Brent held onto Pete, he pushed him back to the ground and slammed into Officer Plitt. Plitt was knocked unconscious and lay there as Pete struggled on top.

Brent's dick was throbbing and screaming to be released from his shorts. Like a madman, while holding Pete to the ground, Brent ripped open his shorts and pulled them to the middle of his beefy, hairy thighs. Pete was still scrambling and wiggling his butt, trying to break free of Brent's hold, but to no avail. As Pete continued to writhe, Brent spat a massive load of saliva into his hand and slurped his throbbing cock until it was shiny and wet. He quickly reached down and shoved two fingers into Pete's bouncing ass. Brent got a look of surprise on his face when he realized that there was already cum and spit inside this man's hole.

Brent couldn't control it anymore. He scooped the cocktail of cum and spit he'd gotten out of Pete's ass, wiped it on his stiff cock, and without any further warning, shoved his cock into Pete's ass. Pete yelled out, and as if he'd turned into a statue, he stopped moving, and his entire body quivered.

With my mouth still full of Marcus's dripping cock, and Marcus twisting my left nipple and still fondling my hard cock, I could turn and see what was happening next to me.

Brent was on top of Pete and deep inside Pete's ass. Pete's body had gone into overdrive, and he was actively grinding his ass up against Brent's every thrust. Pete was held down over the top of Officer Plitt. He began mouthing Officer Plitt's lips while the passed-out trooper lay immobilized.

Suddenly, Marcus pulled out of my mouth, and before I could react, he used his brute strength and flipped me over. He grabbed me by the waist and yanked me over to where Brent, Pete, and the trooper were.

Marcus threw me down, and my head was near Officer Plitt's crotch. I tried to push up, but Marcus was on me before I could make any quick moves. Marcus reached over me, grabbed Officer Plitt's uniform slacks at the waist, and pulled on them until they ripped off his groin. The warm scent of man's sweat, sweaty pubes, dried piss, and a little cologne wafted to my face. No sooner did I get a whiff of that fantastic scent than I felt a hand on the back of my head, and I was shoved down onto Officer Plitt's flaccid cock. I could see the dark, red, kinky pubic hairs on his crotch. Officer Plitt's dick was pink and even had some freckles along the shaft. I could see this before his shaft was embedded inside my mouth.

I tried to pull back but was forced down again. As I tried to pull off Officer Plitt's dick, I suddenly felt a searing pain start shooting from my ass and raging through my groin. I had the feeling of being full inside. As my mind cleared for a few seconds, I realized Marcus had shoved his wet sloppy cock as far into me as he could. I have never been fucked, and all I could think was how full I felt and how much it fucking hurt.

I yelled out, "Stop, motherfucker, STOP!"

Marcus didn't hear me or didn't pay attention. He suddenly pulled his dick out of my ass until only the head was still inside. I breathed for a second, and then my head was shoved back down on Officer Plitt's cock; I gagged and felt the returning pain as Marcus shoved his cock deep inside again.

As I was forcefully spit roasted, I could see Pete licking Officer Plitt's face; then, he began sticking his tongue into the trooper's mouth and swabbing it with his tongue. Pete would groan and grunt while licking the officer's mouth as he was being impaled relentlessly by Brent.

Brent leaned over Pete's back, continued slamming his cock in and out of Pete's ass, and began fighting Pete's mouth and tongue with his own for access to Officer Plitt's mouth, sort of like two rival gangs having a turf war over a prized piece of property.

I felt Marcus's hot breath on my neck as he pressed my mouth over the trooper's hardening dick. He leaned near my ear and said, "You fucking slut, you want my cock, and you will have my cock deep inside you forever." Marcus grunted and slammed into me as hard as he could, and I felt his dick swell inside my broken manhole. Marcus moaned in my ear, "Here it comes, Daddy; your boy is showing you what kind of man he is!" And as he said this, I could feel his cock throbbing and expanding inside my ass. The next thing I felt was the gush of Marcus's man juice as his thick cock rammed shot after shot of cum deep into my hole as my ass muscles spasmed and uncontrollably tried yanking his dick deeper and deeper.

As I felt the hot thickness of Marcus's cum coating the insides of my ass walls, suddenly, Officer Plitt's dick jumped to full attention, throbbed, jerked, and began spewing hot thick strands of pearl-colored cum inside my mouth. I tried swallowing what I could, but some of his cum leaked from my mouth and pooled in the deep red public patch surrounding his dick.

As I sucked the cum out of the state trooper's dick, I saw he had regained consciousness and was now being held and kissed by Brent and Pete. I could see him struggling to try and break free, but with my weight on top of his hips, Marcus on top of me, and Pete and Brent over his chest and face, he was immobilized.

Maybe he saw no other way out, but Officer Plitt seemed to be responding to the kisses he was receiving from the two hot men on top of him.

As I lay there with the state trooper's dick slowly going soft, still sucking some residual cum as his dick retreated, Marcus collapsed on top of me. I could hear his breathing and feel his hot breath on the back of my neck and my ear.

I looked up again and saw Officer Plitt looking back at me as two sets of lips were still assaulting his mouth. Suddenly, Pete pulled back from Officer Plitt. They made eye contact, and Pete gasped. Then, I realized Brent was shooting his load deep into Pete's ass. As Pete's ass was filled with thick spurts of man juice, he leaned back to Officer Plitt and began assaulting his mouth again.

As I lay there basking in the afterglow of this pile of hairy, writhing man meat, I noticed Cliff hanging in his roped position. He was looking at all of us, and his dick throbbed in the evening sunlight. I could see a long strand of cum slowly dripping out of his cock. I glanced below where Cliff hung and noticed a huge wet spot on the ground and realized he had shot a load without even touching his cock. Watching the mass of musky, sweaty, manly men ravaging one another, the drugs he'd been given earlier, and the "skeeter" infection had allowed him to shoot a load by just thinking about it.

We had all forgotten about Roger as Cliff continued to hang and occasionally rock his hips forward and back, and the four of us lay in a sweaty, smelly mound.

Chapter Seventeen

Roger sat in the state trooper's squad car. He watched Officer Plitt slowly and cautiously walk over the hill toward the moonshine still and his workmate.

As he continued to watch, he saw Officer Plitt crouch down as if he was watching something. Before he could react, suddenly he saw his other workmates, Tom and Brent. They came out of the grove of trees behind the hill.

Roger thought, '*Whew, finally, help has arrived.*' But no sooner did he believe that than he remembered how strangely Tom and Brent had acted when he tried to tell them what had happened with him and Cliff.

As he continued to watch, he suddenly saw Brent and Tom move closer to the officer. The next thing he knew, they had wrapped themselves around the state trooper, and the three men had slowly disappeared over the hill. Roger was scared. He had initially felt protected by having the officer here, but now the officer had disappeared. He debated on whether to get out of the cruiser and investigate. He didn't know much about radios and CBs and felt uncomfortable using the equipment in the squad car.

Roger placed his hand on the door latch of the car. He pulled it away. He sat inside the cruiser. The engine had been left running, so he felt comfortable in the air conditioning but still thought he should do something or at least try to see what was happening. He pulled on the door latch, and the door to the cruiser popped open.

Roger put his arm out to push the door open. Suddenly, he heard that strange sound again. That chorus of steel guitar strings screeching in the breeze. He glanced above the police cruiser, and there, right above him, was a brilliant green mass of something squeaking in the air. The group was quivering and folding in upon itself.

As Roger looked, he realized this was part of the same swarm he had seen when he tried to get back to this survey team. He quickly slammed the car door. The swarm swooped down and landed all over the cruiser.

Roger's breath was rushed. He tried to stay calm and thought, '*After all, they were just a bunch of mosquitoes. Right?*' Then he thought again, '*But they sure are a KWEER Skeeter.*'

As Roger sat deep in thought, the sound of one steel guitar shrieked in his ear. Suddenly, Roger felt a hot searing pinch. He reached up and slapped the back of his neck. He pulled his hand down to see what had happened and saw a smashed green insect.

No, it wasn't just an insect; it was a mosquito, but it sure was a KWEER one.

Roger began rocking back and forth, feeling hot waves rush through his body. His dick started to swell uncontrollably. His nipples felt like miniature rockets, ready to shoot into outer space.

Roger placed his hand on the car door again. He absentmindedly caressed the back of his neck. His dick lurched inside his shorts and spewed a thick glob of precum. He pulled the door latch, and the door popped open again.

Roger got out. As he stood, the bulge in his shorts was noticeable, and so was the large wet spot that had quickly begun to show.

As Roger grabbed his throbbing cock, tilted his head back, and rolled his eyes, he took one step forward, and a sexy sneer erupted on his face. He took another step, then another, and slowly, as if in a trance, he walked up and over the small hill, heading toward the moonshine still.

As Roger's figure disappeared over the hill, an orchestra of screeching guitar strings began to sing a twisted and off-key tune…

www.ingramcontent.com/pod-product-compliance
Lightning Source LLC
Chambersburg PA
CBHW070507160726
48003CB00004B/1468